D1200255

Ah, Wilderness!

by Eugene O'Neill

AH, WILDERNESS!

by Eugene O'Neill

With an Introduction by
WALTER KERR

and Illustrations by
SHANNON STIRNWEIS

THE HERITAGE PRESS

Avon, Connecticut

The special contents of this edition are copyright © 1972
by The George Macy Companies, Inc.;
the play copyright 1933 by Eugene O'Neill,
renewed 1960 by Carlotta Monterey O'Neill.
All rights reserved.

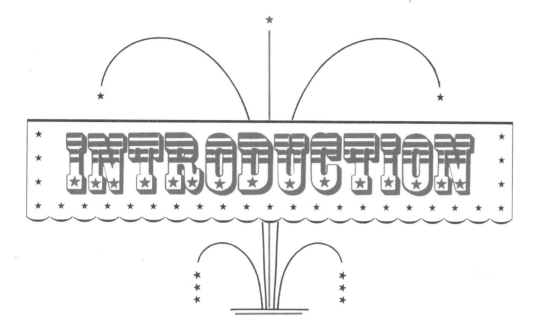

INTRODUCTION

IT IS POSSIBLE that every man remembers two childhoods: the one that he felt and the one that he saw. These two can be quite different, as different as feeling always is from seeing. Of the two, the felt childhood is the stronger, coloring memory for a very long time because it is itself a color, a scent, a set of singing sensations that never did depend upon accurate observation or objective evaluation but instead came directly from the subjective, cradling, buzzing, budding experience of simply being there.

What did it *feel* like to be in an ice-cream parlor, spooning salt-pocked ice cream out of a v-shaped metal container with a swirled cone of paper inside it, sitting on a wire-backed chair that was all open, interlocked curves, feet dangling above a floor like an ocean-wide sea of white tile? You know what it felt like, or at least I do. It felt spacious and light and cool and very, very pure.

Was it? Probably not. You have undoubtedly had the experience of coming upon a photograph, much, much later, of a place you'd ever so clearly remembered. The photograph very likely put you into something close to shock. It recorded a place with some of the features you remembered but not at all in the spatial relationships you thought you remembered; everything may have been more crowded or dingier or busier than it had been in your head. What had not been photographed was the atmosphere the place had had for you, and that couldn't have been photographed because it was *in* you.

Strictly speaking, it isn't necessary to come upon an old photograph. There is also a photograph—quite an exact one—stored somewhere in your head, taken by your eyes at the very same time that your feelings were recording something else. The eyelid shutters blinked, there was a quiet, precise *click!*, a piece of information was filed away.

Feeling and seeing come into being at the same time. They coexist. But they do not coincide. One of them—seeing—is silently tucked away, suppressed and sent to the storehouse by feeling, for future reference or perhaps for no reference at all. For years we get along on treasured sensations, on what we can keep of them; they are a part of us, and help to maintain continuity, even identity. Gradually, though, as our affective powers weaken, as odors and highlights and prickles of the flesh subside and recede, a void opens up. We aren't there any more; that part of us is gone.

And now, if we wish, we can painfully search out the photographs we took; we can rummage about in our brains for information that is there, we can re-place the moment as it was lived with the moment as it was. If I have for a long time treasured how it felt to be walking home from church with my father, side by side (but not hand in hand), and if I now discover that living has gradually dissipated the feeling so that I can no longer enter it wholly, I can do another thing: force my head around front and *see* my father as he was then.

The act is difficult and painful, but I can do it. And I can see that he was not as I felt. He was himself, without me. The objective account is there, some-where, if I care to restore it. Even small children are remarkably good statis-ticians. I can also tell myself that I am now getting closer to the truth, though of course I am only getting closer to another kind of truth. Feeling is just as true as fact; it merely has another kind of content.

Obviously, and at too great length, I am trying to account for something—not something that happened in my own childhood but something that hap-pened in Eugene O'Neill's maturity. O'Neill, in his maturity, first wrote a play called *Ah, Wilderness!* and then, not too long afterward (seven years at most), wrote another called *Long Day's Journey into Night*. Both plays are in some part

autobiographical, the latter almost entirely so, the former surreptitiously so. Both plays have something to do with the youth of Eugene O'Neill. And they could not be farther apart—in tone, in attitude, in intention.

Ah, Wilderness! was always a surprise. From the time that the Theater Guild first produced it in 1933 with George M. Cohan in the role of the young poet's father, O'Neill enthusiasts were stunned. O'Neill had led the American theater's break with its past, with romance and nostalgia and self-admiration and self-deceit. He had looked to New England and found not rock-ribbed virtue but venality of every sort; desire under the elms was incestuous, the wife a man took might be a whore. There were wounds in the world, and Freud peered through them. Abortion and suicide were among O'Neill's first subjects. No one had expected this man to leave room for, or even remember, lazy small-town suppers, cheery Fourth of July celebrations, porches and picnics and virginal daughters on the beach. Suddenly the stage was bathed in a soft though perfectly real moonlight, and a mother and father were kissing in it as the curtain came down. *Ah, Wilderness!* was a warm, fond domestic comedy in which the recent, decent past was very nearly revered. And it did not seem false, coming from this man. It seemed that he had been there.

When, in 1956, *Long Day's Journey into Night* was finally given posthumous production, the surprise of *Ah, Wilderness!* was, retrospectively, even greater. For *Long Day's Journey* is openly a play about O'Neill's family. It presents his mother as a drug addict, his father as a miser, his brother as a drunkard. The boy, Edmond (Eugene), sitting off in a corner taking a thousand mental snapshots each second, was not only suffering from an illness which his father's penuriousness helped bring on, he was the "sensitive" member of the family, the one whose nerve-ends were most ravaged by the violence about him. This childhood—or early manhood—was hell and nothing else.

Yet both plays take place in the same house. Almost everyone who has taken pains to compare the two plays has noticed this, right off. The settings, as described by O'Neill, are interchangeable—the doorways are identical, the windows and the porches and even the rugs on the floor are described with the same adjectives; in both plays there is a central round table with a green-shaded lamp on it, linked by a cord to a chandelier above (in one play the chandelier has four sockets, in the other five). In *imagining* the plays, O'Neill was seeing the same place. Only a change in the lighting could account for a shift in the mood, and that is some time coming. Both plays open with the morning sun streaming in.

Was he seeing the same people? When he was asked this question, during the original run of *Ah, Wilderness!*, O'Neill said not. Though we know now that he had used his own family's living-room, finding both it and the wallpaper design "cheerful," O'Neill claimed that he had drawn the kind of family he would have liked to have had, not the one he did have. And this is backed up by the fact that he borrowed traits, here and there, from the family of a close friend. As all children do at one or another moment in their lives, he idealized the relationships in a neighboring household, yearning for the affection and the solidarity that existed—or seemed to exist—across the street.

And yet no one has ever been able to leave it at that. *Ah, Wilderness!* rings too true to have been all daydream, all envy; looking at it closely, we see that even some of the darker elements of the later play—the more *real* play—have been allowed to enter here, certifying the family experience as his rather than another's; whoring and drunkenness appear, though the whoring is frowned upon and the drunkenness is treated forgivingly.

Clearest of all, though, is the fact that the central thread of the play—its narrative line, its emotional movement—is O'Neill's own personal thread, spun at a time when he was living at home. Richard is the play's principal character: he is O'Neill at a time when O'Neill was reading Swinburne and Wilde and the *Rubaiyat* and that socialist, Shaw. Richard's developing relationship to a virginal neighborhood girl, a "nice" girl named Muriel, is the substance of the play's action: this is unmistakably an echo, a remembrance, of O'Neill's honorable involvement with Maibelle Scott, intelligent and of good family (too good for the likes of young O'Neill, it turned out), to whom he gave books and read poetry and declared his own shy, boyish, innocent passion.

The circumstances are too plain to be wished away. O'Neill was forbidden to continue seeing Maibelle, as Richard is in the play; he continued to see her, courtesy of smuggled notes and clandestine hideaways, as Richard does in the play; the notes were smuggled by a helpful Mildred, though in life Mildred was a friend rather than Richard's sister. The record is more or less complete.

There is just one very strange thing about it. It all happened not when O'Neill was a Richard-innocent of seventeen but when he was a thoroughly experienced young man of twenty-three. It happened *after* O'Neill had been married, become a father, been divorced, whored extensively, attempted suicide. On the face of things, the fact is incredible. Could O'Neill literally have gone through the shy, stammering, impulsive, naive, overly-romantic, in every way boyish ecstasies and despairs he shows Richard going through—at *that* time of his life? He had already *seen* life; he had photographed it for himself. Could he have felt unsullied, adolescent, a gawky greenhorn, a suitor in chivalry's armor?

That, it seems, is exactly what he did feel. Whatever the external facts of his life, he was still inside his life, knew himself in a certain way. His discovery of Maibelle made not only a new but a younger man of him; he turned back and began at a different point; it was possible for him to do so because he had never begun at that point before, he had earlier bypassed it. Puppy love came after callous experience; that is how it happened and O'Neill put it down.

And if O'Neill was able to feel himself Richard because he was able to feel himself in a certain relation to Maibelle—we all sense ourselves differently in relation to different people—might he not also have felt himself Richard in relation to his family? Bear in mind that his romance with Maibelle took place at a time when he was living in that same house with a mother who took morphine and a brother who drank, when he was undergoing the very illness that marks him in *Long Day's Journey*. The source materials for the two plays *do* coincide in time, though O'Neill has shifted some of them out of time to make *Ah, Wilderness!* plausible to the rest of us. Historically speaking, biographically speaking, the Richard who postured and pleaded before Muriel-Maibelle on a moonlit beach is identical with the O'Neill who sat in a corner and saw holo-caust descend.

The gentle, loving, understanding, forgiving family of *Ah, Wilderness!*, then, may be much more nearly O'Neill's own family than O'Neill himself could quite admit. When he was there, when he loved his brother, when he worried for his mother, when he respected his father, he may have felt them as Millers, felt himself a Miller—in part. The truth-telling, the fact-facing of *Long Day's Journey* may have been forced out later, after feeling had been exhausted or after feeling had been honored by the writing of *Ah, Wilderness!* (The exhaus-tion of feeling is suggested by the minor, unparticipating, sit-in-a-corner role O'Neill gives himself when he comes to the photographic documentation, the alienated recording, of the later play; it is as though he were no longer a part of the family, only its objective chronicler.) Perhaps the love is in the first play, and the anguish in the second. But first and second are both true, both personal, both part of the experienced, endlessly complicated, reality.

The same home, very nearly the same people, plainly the same Richard, seen under a different light. That O'Neill could control the lighting of his life as a master electrician controls a switchboard is strongly suggested by Arthur and Barbara Gelb in their definitive biography, *O'Neill.* "Even at twenty," the Gelbs write, "Eugene revealed a paradoxical nature. Vain and egotistical at times, he could also be touchingly helpless. Throughout his life he remained a puzzle to the people who knew him best, for he was given to swift reversals and conveyed sharply different impressions of himself—often deliberately. He was worldly in experience, yet naive in its application to his own life; shy and senti-mental one instant, hard as nails the next; an incipient artist of uncanny insight and sensitivity, yet a man who often misunderstood and failed those who de-pended on him; a victim of self-pity, and a hero challenging the fates."

Which struggle, do you suppose, was more difficult for this man—to pare away nostalgia and let the bleak, harsh facts stand naked under the glare from that overhead chandelier, or to let nostalgia have its say? *Ah, Wilderness!* is the single O'Neill play in which nostalgia, unadulterated affection, helpless fond-

ness are given free rein. It is careful work, mind you, not bathos. The attention to detail, the slow honoring of the rhythm of daily life, the interjection of a dark side even when the mood is at its sunniest, are all the calculated effects of a man conscious of what he is doing. *Ah, Wilderness!* is not O'Neill's day-off, not a vacation, not a self-indulgence, not a whim.

Consider the complete success with which he has managed something extraordinarily difficult. When Sid, the drunken uncle who is loved by spinster Lily, comes home from his picnic celebrations much too much under the weather to keep his promise to take Lily to the evening fireworks, the scene, harrowing as it is for Lily and shaming as it will be to Sid later, has to be funny. It has to make Sid, in his cups, exactly as funny to us as he is to the family. It is his gaiety—his innate humor, his puckish inventiveness—that endears him to everyone and encourages them to tolerate him. A merely predictable drunk, a boorish drunk, would be of no interest to Lily, would not be endurable at the respectable Miller dinner-table. While Sid is drunk and disappointing everyone, O'Neill has got to display Sid's charm, explain why all the youngsters are laughing at him and why even the elders cannot quite keep their faces straight.

It is hard to persuade an audience to laugh when the characters on the stage are laughing; as a rule the demand generates resistance in the audience. But O'Neill has done it so deftly, so lightly, so good-naturedly that we are scarcely aware of the problem. (The fact that O'Neill could sense the light side of drunkenness, even at this remembered time of his life, again hints at the ambivalence of his feelings toward his father and, in particular, his brother.) The artist is in charge of his materials, precisely centering them between sorrow and a giddiness that simply cannot be suppressed.

Having brought this moment off so perfectly, O'Neill is now in possession of a card up his sleeve. When it is young Richard's turn to come home helplessly drunk, who is there to understand *him* and to take care of him? The hung-over, now repentant Sid, absolute master of the situation at hand, the one man in the world to succor a lad in the circumstances. Irony plays about the later scene: innocent Richard is in the very plight Sid has been so ashamed of, Sid is a savior precisely because of his vices, good and bad reverse roles, innocence and guilt interweave until it is difficult to tell one from the other. As Nat Miller has earlier remarked of his son, "You feel, in spite of all his bold talk out of books, that he's so darned innocent inside." You *do* feel that not only about Richard but about Sid, and not only about Sid but about O'Neill—in this play.

Though *Ah, Wilderness!* is an infinitely careful piece of craftsmanship, the later and harsher play, *Long Day's Journey*, obviously took more doing. O'Neill completed it in 1941, after two years' harrowing work, and was so disturbed by the process and so sensitive to the personal qualities of its revelations that he asked his publisher to put it away and not to permit production until some years after his death. He was still not ready to bring to the light the photographs he had taken so long before; they must be delayed, held off, kept hidden. What would they hurt? Feeling.

The love, I would guess, came not only first but easiest.

WALTER KERR

Ah, Wilderness!

A Play in Four Acts

To

GEORGE JEAN NATHAN

who also, once upon a time,
in peg-top trousers went the pace that kills
along the road to ruin

Scenes

Characters

NAT MILLER, *owner of the* Evening Globe

ESSIE, *his wife*

ARTHUR

RICHARD

MILDRED

TOMMY
} *their children*

SID DAVIS, *Essie's brother*

LILY MILLER, *Nat's sister*

DAVID McCOMBER

MURIEL McCOMBER, *his daughter*

WINT SELBY, *a classmate of Arthur's at Yale*

BELLE

NORAH

BARTENDER

SALESMAN

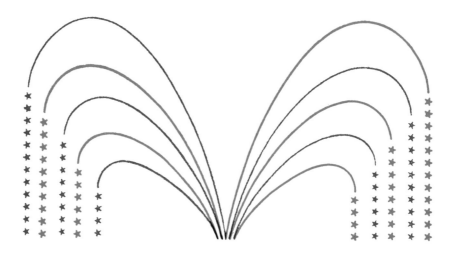

SITTING-ROOM of the Miller home in a large small-town in Connecticut—about 7:30 in the morning of July 4th, 1906.

The room is fairly large, homely looking and cheerful in the morning sunlight, furnished with scrupulous medium-priced tastelessness of the period. Beneath the two windows at left, front, a sofa with silk and satin cushions stands against the wall. At rear of sofa, a bookcase with glass doors, filled with cheap sets, extends along the remaining length of wall. In the rear wall, left, is a double doorway with sliding doors and portières, leading into a dark, windowless, back parlor. At right of this doorway, another bookcase, this time a small open one, crammed with boys' and girls' books and the best-selling novels of many past years—books the family really have read. To the right of this bookcase is the mate of the double doorway at its left, with sliding doors and portières, this one leading to a well-lighted front parlor. In the right wall, rear, a screen door opens on a porch. Farther forward in this wall are two windows, with a writing desk and a chair between them. At center is a big, round table with a green-shaded reading lamp, the cord of the lamp running up to one of five sockets in the chandelier above. Five chairs are grouped about the table—three rockers at left, right, and right rear of it, two armchairs at rear and left rear. A medium-priced, inoffensive rug covers most of the floor. The walls are papered white with a cheerful, ugly blue design.

Voices are heard in a conversational tone from the dining-room beyond the back parlor, where the family are just finishing breakfast. Then MRS. MILLER'*s voice, raised commandingly,* "Tommy! Come back here and finish your milk!" *At the same moment* TOMMY *appears in the doorway from the back parlor—a chubby, sun-burnt boy of eleven with dark eyes, blond hair wetted and plastered down in a part, and a shiny, good-natured face, a rim of milk visible about his lips. Bursting with bottled-up energy and a longing to get started on the Fourth, he nevertheless has hesitated obediently at his mother's call.*

TOMMY (*calls back pleadingly*) Aw, I'm full, Ma. And I said excuse me and you said all right. (*His* FATHER'*s voice is heard speaking to his mother. Then she calls:* "All right, Tommy," *and* TOMMY *asks eagerly*) Can I go out now?

MOTHER'S VOICE (*correctingly*) May I!

TOMMY (*fidgeting, but obediently*) May I, Ma?

MOTHER'S VOICE Yes. (TOMMY *jumps for the screen door to the porch at right like a sprinter released by the starting shot.*)

FATHER'S VOICE (*shouts after him*) But you set off your crackers away from the house, remember! (*But* TOMMY *is already through the screen door, which he leaves open behind him.*)

(*A moment later the family appear from the back parlor, coming from the dining-room. First are* MILDRED *and* ARTHUR. MILDRED *is fifteen, tall and slender, with big, irregular features, resembling her father to the complete effacing of any pretense at prettiness. But her big, gray eyes are beautiful; she has vivacity and a fetching smile, and everyone thinks of her as an attractive girl. She is dressed in shirtwaist and skirt in the fashion of the period.*)

(ARTHUR, *the eldest of the Miller children who are still living home, is nineteen. He is tall, heavy, barrel-chested, and muscular, the type of football linesman of that period, with a square, stolid face, small blue eyes, and thick sandy hair. His manner is solemnly collegiate. He is dressed in the latest college fashion of that day, which has receded a bit from the extreme of preceding years, but still runs to padded shoulders and pants half-pegged at the top, and so small at their wide-cuffed bottoms that they cannot be taken off with shoes on.*)

MILDRED (*as they appear—inquisitively*) Where are you going today, Art?

ARTHUR (*with superior dignity*) That's my business. (*He ostentatiously takes from his pocket a tobacco pouch with a big Υ and class numerals stamped on it, and a heavy bulldog briar pipe with silver Υ and numerals, and starts filling the pipe.*)

MILDRED (*teasingly*) Bet I know, just the same! Want me to tell you her initials? E.R.! (*She laughs.* ARTHUR, *pleased by this insinuation at his lady-killing activities, yet finds it beneath his dignity to reply. He goes to the table, lights his pipe and picks up the local morning paper, and slouches back into the armchair at left rear of table, beginning to whistle "Oh, Waltz Me Around Again, Willie" as he scans the headlines.* MILDRED *sits on the sofa at left, front.*)

(*Meanwhile, their mother and their* AUNT LILY, *their father's sister, have appeared, following them from the back parlor.* MRS. MILLER *is around fifty, a short, stout woman with fading light-brown hair sprinkled with gray, who must have been decidedly pretty as a girl in a round-faced, cute, small-featured, wide-eyed fashion. She has big brown eyes, soft and maternal—a bustling, mother-of-a-family manner. She is dressed in shirtwaist and skirt.*)

(LILY MILLER, *her sister-in-law, is forty-two, tall, dark, and thin. She conforms outwardly to the conventional type of old-maid schoolteacher, even to wearing glasses. But behind the glasses her gray eyes are gentle and tired, and her whole atmosphere is one of shy kindliness. Her voice presents the greatest contrast to her appearance—soft and full of sweetness. She, also, is dressed in a shirtwaist and skirt.*)

MRS. MILLER *(as they appear)* Getting milk down him is like—(*Suddenly she is aware of the screen door standing half open.*) Goodness, look at that door he's left open! The house will be alive with flies! (*Rushing out to shut it*) I've told him again and again—and that's all the good it does! It's just a waste of breath! (*She slams the door shut.*)

LILY *(smiling)* Well, you can't expect a boy to remember to shut doors—on the Fourth of July. (*She goes diffidently to the straight-backed chair before the desk at right, front, leaving the comfortable chairs to the others.*)

MRS. MILLER That's you all over, Lily—always making excuses for him. You'll have him spoiled to death in spite of me. (*She sinks in rocker at right of table.*) Phew, I'm hot, aren't you? This is going to be a scorcher. (*She picks up a magazine from the table and begins to rock, fanning herself.*)

(*Meanwhile, her husband and her brother have appeared from the back parlor, both smoking cigars.* NAT MILLER *is in his late fifties, a tall, dark, spare man, a little stoop-shouldered, more than a little bald, dressed with an awkward attempt at sober respectability imposed upon an innate heedlessness of clothes. His long face has large, irregular, undistinguished features, but he has fine, shrewd, humorous gray eyes.*)

(SID DAVIS, *his brother-in-law, is forty-five, short and fat, bald-headed, with the puckish face of a Peck's Bad Boy who has never grown up. He is dressed in what had once been a very natty loud light suit but is now a shapeless and faded nondescript in cut and color.*)

SID (*as they appear*) Oh, I like the job first rate, Nat. Waterbury's a nifty old town with the lid off, when you get to know the ropes. I rang in a joke in one of my stories that tickled the folks there pink. Waterwagon—Waterbury—Waterloo!

MILLER (*grinning*) Darn good!

SID (*pleased*) I thought it was pretty fair myself. (*Goes on a bit ruefully, as if oppressed by a secret sorrow.*) Yes, you can see life in Waterbury, all right—that is, if you're looking for life in Waterbury!

MRS. MILLER What's that about Waterbury, Sid?

SID I was saying it's all right in its way—but there's no place like home. (*As if to punctuate this remark, there begins a series of bangs from just beyond the porch outside, as TOMMY inaugurates his celebration by setting off a package of firecrackers. The assembled family jump in their chairs.*)

MRS. MILLER That boy! (*She rushes to the screen door and out on the porch, calling*) Tommy! You mind what your Pa told you! You take your crackers out in the back yard, you hear me!

ARTHUR (*frowning scornfully*) Fresh kid! He did it on purpose to scare us.

MILLER (*grinning through his annoyance*) Darned youngster! He'll have the house afire before the day's out.

SID   (*grins and sings*)

> "Dunno what ter call 'im
> But he's mighty like a Rose—velt."

(*They all laugh.*)

LILY   Sid, you Crazy! (SID *beams at her.* MRS. MILLER *comes back from the porch, still fuming.*)

MRS. MILLER   Well, I've made him go out back at last. Now we'll have a little peace. (*As if to contradict this, the bang of firecrackers and torpedoes begins from the rear of the house, left, and continues at intervals throughout the scene, not nearly so loud as the first explosion, but sufficiently emphatic to form a disturbing punctuation to the conversation.*)

MILLER   Well, what's on the tappee for all of you today? Sid, you're coming to the Sachem Club picnic with me, of course.

SID   (*a bit embarrassedly*) You bet. I mean I'd like to, Nat—that is, if—

MRS. MILLER   (*regarding her brother with smiling suspicion*) Hmm! I know what that Sachem Club picnic's always meant!

LILY   (*breaks in in a forced joking tone that conceals a deep earnestness*) No, not this time, Essie. Sid's a reformed character since he's been on the paper in Waterbury. At least, that's what he swore to me last night.

SID   (*avoiding her eyes, humiliated—joking it off*) Pure as the driven snow, that's me. They're running me for president of the W.C.T.U. (*They all laugh.*)

MRS. MILLER   Sid, you're a caution. You turn everything into a joke. But you be careful, you hear? We're going to have dinner in the evening tonight, you know—the best shore dinner you ever tasted and I don't want you coming home—well, not able to appreciate it.

LILY Oh, I know he'll be careful today. Won't you, Sid?

SID (*more embarrassed than ever—joking it off melodramatically*) Lily, I swear to you if any man offers me a drink, I'll kill him—that is, if he changes his mind! (*They all laugh except* LILY, *who bites her lip and stiffens.*)

MRS. MILLER No use talking to him, Lily. You ought to know better by this time. We can only hope for the best.

MILLER Now, you women stop picking on Sid. It's the Fourth of July and even a downtrodden newspaperman has a right to enjoy himself when he's on his holiday.

MRS. MILLER I wasn't thinking only of Sid.

MILLER (*with a wink at the others*) What, are you insinuating I ever—?

MRS. MILLER Well, to do you justice, no, not what you'd really call—But I've known you to come back from this darned Sachem Club picnic —Well, I didn't need any little bird to whisper that you'd been some place besides to the well! (*She smiles good-naturedly.* MILLER *chuckles.*)

SID (*after a furtive glance at the stiff and silent* LILY—*changes the subject abruptly by turning to* ARTHUR) How are you spending the festive Fourth, Boola-Boola? (ARTHUR *stiffens dignifiedly.*)

MILDRED (*teasingly*) I can tell you, if he won't.

MRS. MILLER (*smiling*) Off to the Rands', I suppose.

ARTHUR (*with dignity*) I and Bert Turner are taking Elsie and Ethel Rand canoeing. We're going to have a picnic lunch on Strawberry Island. And this evening I'm staying at the Rands' for dinner.

MILLER You're accounted for, then. How about you, Mid?

MILDRED I'm going to the beach to Anne Culver's.

ARTHUR (*sarcastically*) Of course, there won't be any boys present! Johnny Dodd, for example?

MILDRED (*giggles—then with a coquettish toss of her head*) Pooh! What do I care for him? He's not the only pebble on the beach.

MILLER Stop your everlasting teasing, you two. How about you and Lily, Essie?

MRS. MILLER I don't know. I haven't made any plans, have you, Lily?

LILY (*quietly*) No. Anything you want to do.

MRS. MILLER Well, I thought we'd just sit around and rest and talk.

MILLER You can gossip any day. This is the Fourth. Now, I've got a better suggestion than that. What do you say to an automobile ride? I'll get out the Buick and we'll drive around town and out to the lighthouse and back. Then Sid and I will let you off here, or anywhere you say, and we'll go on to the picnic.

MRS. MILLER I'd love it. Wouldn't you, Lily?

LILY It would be nice.

MILLER Then, that's all settled.

SID (*embarrassedly*) Lily, want to come with me to the fireworks display at the beach tonight?

MRS. MILLER That's right, Sid. You take her out. Poor Lily never has any fun, always sitting home with me.

LILY (*flustered and grateful*) I—I'd like to, Sid, thank you. (*Then an apprehensive look comes over her face.*) Only not if you come home—you know.

SID (*again embarrassed and humiliated—again joking it off, solemnly*) Evil-minded, I'm afraid, Nat. I hate to say it of your sister. (*They all laugh. Even* LILY *cannot suppress a smile.*)

ARTHUR (*with heavy jocularity*) Listen, Uncle Sid. Don't let me catch you and Aunt Lily spooning on a bench tonight—or it'll be my duty to call a cop! (SID *and* LILY *both look painfully embarrassed at this, and the joke falls flat, except for* MILDRED *who can't restrain a giggle at the thought of these two ancients spooning.*)

MRS. MILLER (*rebukingly*) Arthur!

MILLER (*dryly*) That'll do you. Your education in kicking a football around Yale seems to have blunted your sense of humor.

MRS. MILLER (*suddenly—startledly*) But where's Richard? We're forgetting all about him. Why, where is that boy? I thought he came in with us from breakfast.

MILDRED I'll bet he's off somewhere writing a poem to Muriel McComber, the silly! Or pretending to write one. I think he just copies—

ARTHUR (*looking back toward the dining-room*) He's still in the dining-room, reading a book. (*Turning back—scornfully*) Gosh, he's always reading now. It's not my idea of having a good time in vacation.

MILLER (*caustically*) He read his school books, too, strange as that may seem to you. That's why he came out top of his class. I'm hoping before you leave New Haven they'll find time to teach you reading is a good habit.

MRS. MILLER (*sharply*) That reminds me, Nat. I've been meaning to speak to you about those awful books Richard is reading. You've got to give him a good talking to—(*She gets up from her chair.*) I'll go up and get them right now. I found them where he'd hid them on the shelf in his wardrobe. You just wait till you see what—(*She bustles off, rear right, through the front parlor.*)

MILLER (*plainly not relishing whatever is coming—to* SID, *grumblingly*) Seems to me she might wait until the Fourth is over before bringing up—(*Then with a grin*) I know there's nothing to it, anyway. When I think of the books I used to sneak off and read when I was a kid.

SID Me, too. I suppose Dick is deep in Nick Carter or Old Cap Collier.

MILLER No, he passed that period long ago. Poetry's his red meat nowadays, I think—love poetry—and socialism, too, I suspect, from some dire declarations he's made. (*Then briskly*) Well, might as well get him on the carpet. (*He calls*) Richard. (*No answer— louder*) Richard. (*No answer—then in a bellow*) Richard!

ARTHUR (*shouting*) Hey, Dick, wake up! Pa's calling you.

RICHARD'S VOICE (*from the dining-room*) All right. I'm coming.

MILLER Darn him! When he gets his nose in a book, the house could fall down and he'd never—

(RICHARD *appears in the doorway from the back parlor, the book he has been reading in one hand, a finger marking his place. He looks a bit startled still, reluctantly called back to earth from another world.*)

(*He is going on seventeen, just out of high school. In appearance he is a perfect blend of father and mother, so much so that each is convinced he is the image of the other. He has his mother's lightbrown hair, his father's gray eyes; his features are neither large nor small; he is of medium height, neither fat nor thin. One would not call him a handsome boy; neither is he homely. But he is definitely different from both of his parents, too. There is something of extreme sensitiveness added—a restless, apprehensive, defiant, shy, dreamy, self-conscious intelligence about him. In manner he is alternately plain simple boy and a posey actor solemnly playing a role. He is dressed in prep school reflection of the college style of* ARTHUR.)

RICHARD Did you want me, Pa?

MILLER I'd hoped I'd made that plain. Come and sit down a while. (*He points to the rocking-chair at the right of table near his.*)

RICHARD (*coming forward—seizing on the opportunity to play up his pre-occupation—with apologetic superiority*) I didn't hear you, Pa. I was off in another world. (MILDRED *slyly shoves her foot out so that he trips over it, almost falling. She laughs gleefully. So does* ARTHUR.)

ARTHUR Good for you, Mid! That'll wake him up!

RICHARD (*grins sheepishly—all boy now*) Darn you, Mid! I'll show you!

(*He pushes her back on the sofa and tickles her with his free hand, still holding the book in the other. She shrieks.*)

ARTHUR Give it to her, Dick!

MILLER That's enough, now. No more roughhouse. You sit down here, Richard. (RICHARD *obediently takes the chair at right of table, opposite his father.*) What were you planning to do with yourself today? Going out to the beach with Mildred?

RICHARD (*scornfully superior*) That silly skirt party! I should say not!

MILDRED He's not coming because Muriel isn't. I'll bet he's got a date with her somewheres.

RICHARD (*flushing bashfully*) You shut up! (*Then to his father*) I thought I'd just stay home, Pa—this morning, anyway.

MILLER Help Tommy set off firecrackers, eh?

RICHARD (*drawing himself up—with dignity*) I should say not. (*Then frowning portentously*) I don't believe in this silly celebrating the Fourth of July—all this lying talk about liberty—when there is no liberty!

MILLER (*a twinkle in his eye*) Hmm.

RICHARD (*getting warmed up*) The land of the free and the home of the brave! Home of the slave is what they ought to call it—the wage slave ground under the heel of the capitalist class, starving, crying for bread for his children, and all he gets is a stone! The Fourth of July is a stupid farce!

MILLER (*putting a hand to his mouth to conceal a grin*) Hmm. Them are mighty strong words. You'd better not repeat such sentiments outside the bosom of the family or they'll have you in jail.

SID And throw away the key.

RICHARD (*darkly*) Let them put me in jail. But how about the freedom of speech in the Constitution, then? That must be a farce, too. (*Then he adds grimly*) No, you can celebrate your Fourth of July. I'll celebrate the day the people bring out the guillotine again and I see Pierpont Morgan being driven by in a tumbril! (*His father and* SID *are greatly amused;* LILY *is shocked but, taking her cue from them, smiles.* MILDRED *stares at him in puzzled wonderment, never having heard this particular line before. Only* ARTHUR *betrays the outraged reaction of a patriot.*)

ARTHUR Aw say, you fresh kid, tie that bull outside! You ought to get a punch in the nose for talking that way on the Fourth!

MILLER (*solemnly*) Son, if I didn't know it was you talking, I'd think we had Emma Goldman with us.

ARTHUR Never mind, Pa. Wait till we get him down to Yale. We'll take that out of him!

RICHARD   (*with high scorn*) Oh, Yale! You think there's nothing in the world besides Yale. After all, what is Yale?

ARTHUR   You'll find out what!

SID   (*provocatively*) Don't let them scare you, Dick. Give 'em hell!

LILY   (*shocked*) Sid! You shouldn't swear before—

RICHARD   What do you think I am, Aunt Lily—a baby? I've heard worse than anything Uncle Sid says.

MILDRED   And said worse himself, I bet!

MILLER   (*with a comic air of resignation*) Well, Richard, I've always found I've had to listen to at least one stump speech every Fourth. I only hope getting your extra strong one right after breakfast will let me off for the rest of the day. (*They all laugh now, taking this as a cue.*)

RICHARD   (*somberly*) That's right, laugh! After you, the deluge, you think! But look out! Supposing it comes before? Why shouldn't the workers of the world unite and rise? They have nothing to lose but their chains! (*He recites threateningly*) "The days grow hot, O Babylon! 'Tis cool beneath thy willow trees!"

MILLER   Hmm. That's good. But where's the connection, exactly? Something from that book you're reading?

RICHARD   (*superior*) No. That's poetry. This is prose.

MILLER   I've heard there was a difference between 'em. What is the book?

RICHARD   (*importantly*) Carlyle's "French Revolution."

MILLER   Hmm. So that's where you drove the tumbril from and piled poor old Pierpont in it. (*Then seriously*) Glad you're reading it, Richard. It's a darn fine book.

RICHARD (*with unflattering astonishment*) What, have you read it?

MILLER Well, you see, even a newspaper owner can't get out of reading a book every now and again.

RICHARD (*abashed*) I—I didn't mean—I know you—(*Then enthusiastically*) Say, isn't it a great book, though—that part about Mirabeau—and about Marat and Robespierre—

MRS. MILLER (*appears from the front parlor in a great state of flushed annoyance*) Never you mind Robespierre, young man! You tell me this minute where you've hidden those books! They were on the shelf in your wardrobe and now you've gone and hid them somewhere else. You go right up and bring them to your father! (RICHARD, *for a second, looks suddenly guilty and crushed. Then he bristles defensively.*)

MILLER (*after a quick understanding glance at him*) Never mind his getting them now. We'll waste the whole morning over those darned books. And anyway, he has a right to keep his library to himself—that is, if they're not too—What books are they, Richard?

RICHARD (*self-consciously*) Well—there's—

MRS. MILLER I'll tell you, if he won't—and you give him a good talking to. (*Then, after a glance at* RICHARD, *mollifiedly*) Not that I blame Richard. There must be some boy he knows who's trying to show off as advanced and wicked, and he told him about—

RICHARD No! I read about them myself, in the papers and in other books.

MRS. MILLER Well, no matter how, there they were on his shelf. Two by that awful Oscar Wilde they put in jail for heaven knows what wickedness.

ARTHUR (*suddenly—solemnly authoritative*) He committed bigamy. (*Then as* SID *smothers a burst of ribald laughter*) What are you laughing at? I guess I ought to know. A fellow at college told me. His father was in England when this Wilde was pinched—and he said he remembered once his mother asked his father about it and he told her he'd committed bigamy.

MILLER (*hiding a smile behind his hand*) Well then, that must be right, Arthur.

MRS. MILLER I wouldn't put it past him, nor anything else. One book was called the Picture of something or other.

RICHARD "The Picture of Dorian Gray." It's one of the greatest novels ever written!

MRS. MILLER Looked to me like cheap trash. And the second book was poetry. The Ballad of I forget what.

RICHARD "The Ballad of Reading Gaol," one of the greatest poems ever written. (*He pronounces it Reading Goal [as in goalpost].*)

MRS. MILLER All about someone who murdered his wife and got hung, as he richly deserved, as far as I could make out. And then there were two books by that Bernard Shaw—

RICHARD The greatest playwright alive today!

MRS. MILLER To hear him tell it, maybe! You know, Nat, the one who wrote a play about—well, never mind—that was so vile they wouldn't even let it play in New York!

MILLER Hmm. I remember.

MRS. MILLER One was a book of his plays and the other had a long title I couldn't make head or tail of, only it wasn't a play.

RICHARD (*proudly*) "The Quintessence of Ibsenism."

MILDRED   Phew! Good gracious, what a name! What does it mean, Dick? I'll bet he doesn't know.

RICHARD   (*outraged*) I do, too, know! It's about Ibsen, the greatest playwright since Shakespeare!

MRS. MILLER   Yes, there was a book of plays by that Ibsen there, too! And poems by Swin something—

RICHARD   "Poems and Ballads" by Swinburne, Ma. The greatest poet since Shelley! He tells the truth about real love!

MRS. MILLER   Love! Well, all I can say is, from reading here and there, that if he wasn't flung in jail along with Wilde, he should have been. Some of the things I simply couldn't read, they were so indecent —All about—well, I can't tell you before Lily and Mildred.

SID   (*with a wink at* RICHARD—*jokingly*) Remember, I'm next on that one, Dick. I feel the need of a little poetical education.

LILY   (*scandalized, but laughing*) Sid! Aren't you ashamed?

MRS. MILLER   This is no laughing matter. And then there was Kipling—but I suppose he's not so bad. And last there was a poem—a long one —the Rubay—What is it, Richard?

RICHARD   "The Rubaiyat of Omar Khayyam." That's the best of all!

MILLER   Oh, I've read that, Essie—got a copy down at the office.

SID   (*enthusiastically*) So have I. It's a pippin!

LILY   (*with shy excitement*) I—I've read it, too—at the library. I like —some parts of it.

MRS. MILLER   (*scandalized*) Why, Lily!

MILLER   Everybody's reading that now, Essie—and it don't seem to do them any harm. There's fine things in it, seems to me—true things.

MRS. MILLER (*a bit bewildered and uncertain now*) Why, Nat, I don't see how you—It looked terrible blasphemous—parts I read.

SID Remember this one (*He quotes rhetorically*) "Oh Thou, who didst with pitfall and gin beset the path I was to wander in—" Now, I've always noticed how beset my path was with gin—in the past, you understand! (*He casts a joking side glance at* LILY. *The others laugh. But* LILLY *is in a melancholy dream and hasn't heard him.*)

MRS. MILLER (*tartly, but evidently suppressing her usual smile where he is concerned*) You would pick out the ones with liquor in them!

LILY (*suddenly—with a sad pathos, quotes awkwardly and shyly*) I like—because it's true:

> "The Moving Finger writes, and having writ,
> Moves on: nor all your Piety nor Wit
> Shall lure it back to cancel half a Line,
> Nor all your Tears wash out a Word of it."

MRS. MILLER (*astonished, as are all the others*) Why, Lily, I never knew you to recite poetry before!

LILY (*immediately guilty and apologetic*) I—it just stuck in my memory somehow.

RICHARD (*looking at her as if he had never seen her before*) Good for you, Aunt Lily! (*Then enthusiastically*) But that isn't the best. The best is:

> "A Book of Verses underneath the Bough,
> A Jug of Wine, a Loaf of Bread—and Thou
> Beside me singing in the Wilderness—"

ARTHUR (*who, bored to death by all this poetry quoting, has wandered over to the window at rear of desk, right*) Hey! Look who's coming up the walk—Old Man McComber!

MILLER (*irritably*) Dave? Now what in thunder does that damned old— Sid, I can see where we never are going to get to that picnic.

MRS. MILLER (*vexatiously*) He'll know we're in this early, too. No use lying. (*Then appalled by another thought*) That Norah—she's that thick, she never can answer the front door right unless I tell her each time. Nat, you've got to talk to Dave. I'll have her show him in here. Lily, you run up the back stairs and get your things on. I'll be up in a second. Nat, you get rid of him the first second you can! Whatever can the old fool want—(*She and* LILY *hurry out through the back parlor.*)

ARTHUR I'm going to beat it—just time to catch the eight-twenty trolley.

MILDRED I've got to catch that, too. Wait till I get my hat, Art! (*She rushes into the back parlor.*)

ARTHUR (*shouts after her*) I can't wait. You can catch up with me if you hurry. (*He turns at the back-parlor door—with a grin*) McComber may be coming to see if your intentions toward his daughter are dishonorable, Dick! You'd better beat it while your shoes are good! (*He disappears through the back-parlor door, laughing.*)

RICHARD (*a bit shaken, but putting on a brave front*) Think I'm scared of him?

MILLER (*gazing at him—frowning*) Can't imagine what—But it's to complain about something, I know that. I only wish I didn't have to be pleasant with the old buzzard—but he's about the most valuable advertiser I've got.

SID (*sympathetically*) I know. But tell him to go to hell, anyway. He needs that ad more than you.

(*The sound of the bell comes from the rear of the house, off left from back parlor.*)

MILLER   There he is. You clear out, Dick—but come right back as soon as he's gone, you hear? I'm not through with you, yet.

RICHARD   Yes, Pa.

MILLER   You better clear out, too, Sid. You know Dave doesn't approve of jokes.

SID   And loves me like poison! Come on, Dick, we'll go out and help Tommy celebrate. (*He takes* RICHARD's *arm and they also disappear through the back-parlor door.* MILLER *glances through the front parlor toward the front door, then calls in a tone of strained heartiness.*)

MILLER   Hello, Dave. Come right in here. What good wind blows you around on this glorious Fourth?
(*A flat, brittle voice answers him: "Good morning," and a moment later* DAVID MC COMBER *appears in the doorway from the front parlor. He is a thin, dried-up little man with a head too large for his body perched on a scrawny neck, and a long solemn horse face with deep-set little black eyes, a blunt formless nose, and a tiny slit of a mouth. He is about the same age as* MILLER *but is entirely bald, and looks ten years older. He is dressed with a prim neatness in shiny old black clothes.*)

MILLER   Here, sit down and make yourself comfortable. (*Holding out the cigar box*) Have a cigar?

MC COMBER   (*sitting down in the chair at the right of table—acidly*) You're forgetting. I never smoke.

MILLER   (*forcing a laugh at himself*) That's so. So I was. Well, I'll smoke alone then. (*He bites off the end of the cigar viciously, as if he wished it were* MC COMBER's *head, and sits down opposite him.*)

MC COMBER   You asked me what brings me here, so I'll come to the point at once. I regret to say it's something disagreeable—disgraceful would be nearer the truth—and it concerns your son, Richard!

MILLER *(beginning to bristle—but calmly)* Oh, come now, Dave, I'm sure Richard hasn't—

MC COMBER *(sharply)* And I'm positive he has. You're not accusing me of being a liar, I hope.

MILLER No one said anything about liar. I only meant you're surely mistaken if you think—

MC COMBER I'm not mistaken. I have proof of everything in his own handwriting!

MILLER *(sharply)* Let's get down to brass tacks. Just what is it you're charging him with?

MC COMBER With being dissolute and blasphemous—with deliberately attempting to corrupt the morals of my young daughter, Muriel.

MILLER Then I'm afraid I will have to call you a liar, Dave!

MC COMBER *(without taking offense—in the same flat, brittle voice)* I thought you'd get around to that, so I brought some of the proofs with me. I've a lot more of 'em at home. *(He takes a wallet from his inside coat pocket, selects five or six slips of paper, and holds them out to* MILLER.*)* These are good samples of the rest. My wife discovered them in one of Muriel's bureau drawers hidden under the underwear. They're all in his handwriting, you can't deny it. Anyway, Muriel's confessed to me he wrote them. You read them and then say I'm a liar. *(*MILLER *has taken the slips and is reading them frowningly.* MC COMBER *talks on)* Evidently you've been too busy to take the right care about Richard's bringing up or what he's allowed to read—though I can't see why his mother failed in her duty. But that's your misfortune, and none of my business. But Muriel is my business and I can't and I won't have her innocence exposed to the contamination of a young man whose mind, judging from his choice of reading matter, is as foul—

MILLER (*making a tremendous effort to control his temper*) Why, you damned old fool! Can't you see Richard's only a fool kid who's just at the stage when he's out to rebel against all authority, and so he grabs at everything radical to read and wants to pass it on to his elders and his girl and boy friends to show off what a young hellion he is! Why, at heart you'd find Richard is just as innocent and as big a kid as Muriel is! (*He pushes the slips of paper across the table contemptuously.*) This stuff doesn't mean anything to me—that is, nothing of what you think it means. If you believe this would corrupt Muriel, then you must believe she's easily corrupted! But I'll bet you'd find she knows a lot more about life than you give her credit for—and can guess a stork didn't bring her down your chimney!

MC COMBER Now you're insulting my daughter. I won't forget that.

MILLER I'm not insulting her. I think Muriel is a darn nice girl. That's why I'm giving her credit for ordinary good sense. I'd say the same about my own Mildred, who's the same age.

MC COMBER I know nothing about your Mildred except that she's known all over as a flirt. (*Then more sharply*) Well, I knew you'd prove obstinate, but I certainly never dreamed you'd have the impudence, after reading those papers, to claim your son was innocent of all wrong-doing!

MILLER And what did you dream I'd do?

MC COMBER Do what it's your plain duty to do as a citizen to protect other people's children! Take and give him a hiding he'd remember to the last day of his life! You'd ought to do it for his sake, if you had any sense—unless you want him to end up in jail!

MILLER (*his fists clenched, leans across the table*) Dave, I've stood all I can stand from you! You get out! And get out quick, if you don't want a kick in the rear to help you!

MC COMBER (*again in his flat, brittle voice, slowly getting to his feet*) You needn't lose your temper. I'm only demanding you do your duty by your own as I've already done by mine. I'm punishing Muriel. She's not to be allowed out of the house for a month and she's to be in bed every night by eight sharp. And yet she's blameless, compared to that—

MILLER I said I'd had enough out of you, Dave! (*He makes a threatening movement.*)

MC COMBER You needn't lay hands on me. I'm going. But there's one thing more. (*He takes a letter from his wallet.*) Here's a letter from Muriel for your son. (*Puts it on the table.*) It makes clear, I think, how she's come to think about him, now that her eyes have been opened. I hope he heeds what's inside—for his own good and yours—because if I ever catch him hanging about my place again I'll have him arrested! And don't think I'm not going to make you regret the insults you've heaped on me. I'm taking the advertisement for my store out of your paper—and it won't go in again, I tell you, not unless you apologize in writing and promise to punish—

MILLER I'll see you in hell first! As for your damned old ad, take it out and go to hell!

MC COMBER That's plain bluff. You know how badly you need it. So do I. (*He starts stiffly for the door.*)

MILLER Here! Listen a minute! I'm just going to call *your* bluff and tell you that, whether you want to reconsider your decision or not, I'm going to refuse to print your damned ad after tomorrow! Put that in your pipe and smoke it! Furthermore, I'll start a campaign to encourage outside capital to open a dry-goods store in opposition to you that won't be the public swindle I can prove yours is!

MC COMBER (*a bit shaken by this threat—but in the same flat tone*) I'll sue you for libel.

MILLER When I get through, there won't be a person in town will buy a dishrag in your place!

MC COMBER (*more shaken, his eyes shifting about furtively*) That's all bluff. You wouldn't dare— (*Then finally he says uncertainly*) Well, good day. (*And turns and goes out.* NAT *stands looking after him. Slowly the anger drains from his face and leaves him looking a bit sick and disgusted.* SID *appears from the back parlor. He is nursing a burn on his right hand, but his face is one broad grin of satisfaction.*)

SID I burned my hand with one of Tommy's damned firecrackers and came in to get some vaseline. I was listening to the last of your scrap. Good for you, Nat! You sure gave him hell!

MILLER (*dully*) Much good it'll do. He knows it was all talk.

SID That's just what he don't know, Nat. The old skinflint has a guilty conscience.

MILLER Well, anyone who knows me knows I wouldn't use my paper for a dirty, spiteful trick like that—no matter what he did to me.

SID Yes, everyone knows you're an old sucker, Nat, too decent for your own good. But McComber never saw you like this before. I tell you you scared the pants off him. (*He chuckles.*)

MILLER   (*still dejectedly*) I don't know what made me let go like that. The hell of skunks like McComber is that after being with them ten minutes you become as big skunks as they are.

SID   (*notices the slips of paper on the table*) What's this? Something he brought? (*He picks them up and starts to read.*)

MILLER   (*grimly*) Samples of the new freedom—from those books Essie found—that Richard's been passing on to Muriel to educate her. They're what started the rumpus. (*Then frowning*) I've got to do something about that young anarchist or he'll be getting me, and himself, in a peck of trouble. (*Then pathetically helpless*) But what can I do? Putting the curb bit on would make him worse. Then he'd have a harsh tyrant to defy. He'd love that, darn him!

SID   (*has been reading the slips, a broad grin on his face—suddenly he whistles*) Phew! This is a warm lulu for fair! (*He recites with a joking intensity*)

> "My life is bitter with thy love; thine eyes
>   Blind me, thy tresses burn me, thy sharp sighs
>   Divide my flesh and spirit with soft sound—"

MILLER   (*with a grim smile*) Hmm. I missed that one. That must be Mr. Swinburne's copy. I've never read him, but I've heard something like that was the matter with him.

SID   Yes, it's labelled Swinburne—"Anactoria." Whatever that is. But wait, watch and listen! The worst is yet to come! (*He recites with added comic intensity*)

> "That I could drink thy veins as wine, and eat
>   Thy breasts like honey, that from face to feet
>   Thy body were abolished and consumed,
>   And in my flesh thy very flesh entombed!"

MILLER *(an irrepressible boyish grin coming to his face)* Hell and halle-lujah! Just picture old Dave digesting that for the first time! Gosh, I'd give a lot to have seen his face! *(Then a trace of shocked reproof showing in his voice)* But it's no joking matter. That stuff *is* warm—too damned warm, if you ask me! I don't like this a damned bit, Sid. That's no kind of thing to be sending a decent girl. *(More worriedly)* I thought he was really stuck on her—as one gets stuck on a decent girl at his age—all moonshine and holding hands and a kiss now and again. But this looks—I wonder if he is hanging around her to see what he can get? *(Angrily)* By God, if that's true, he deserves that licking Mc-Comber says it's my duty to give him! I've got to draw the line somewhere!

SID Yes, it won't do to have him getting any decent girl in trouble.

MILLER The only thing I can do is put it up to him straight. *(With pride)* Richard'll stand up to his guns, no matter what. I've never known him to lie to me.

SID *(at a noise from the back parlor, looks that way—in a whisper)* Then now's your chance. I'll beat it and leave you alone—see if the women folks are ready upstairs. We ought to get started soon—if we're ever going to make that picnic. *(He is halfway to the entrance to the front parlor as* RICHARD *enters from the back parlor, very evidently nervous about* MC COMBER's *call.)*

RICHARD *(adopting a forced, innocent tone)* How's your hand, Uncle Sid?

SID All right, Dick, thanks—only hurts a little. *(He disappears.* MILLER *watches his son frowningly.* RICHARD *gives him a quick side glance and grows more guiltily self-conscious.)*

RICHARD (*forcing a snicker*) Gee, Pa, Uncle Sid's a bigger kid than Tommy is. He was throwing firecrackers in the air and catching them on the back of his hand and throwing 'em off again just before they went off—and one came and he wasn't quick enough, and it went off almost on top of—

MILLER Never mind that. I've got something else to talk to you about besides firecrackers.

RICHARD (*apprehensively*) What, Pa?

MILLER (*suddenly puts both hands on his shoulders—quietly*) Look here, Son. I'm going to ask you a question, and I want an honest answer. I warn you beforehand if the answer is "yes" I'm going to punish you and punish you hard because you'll have done something no boy of mine ought to do. But you've never lied to me before, I know, and I don't believe, even to save yourself punishment, you'd lie to me now, would you?

RICHARD (*impressed—with dignity*) I won't lie, Pa.

MILLER Have you been trying to have something to do with Muriel—something you shouldn't—you know what I mean.

RICHARD (*stares at him for a moment, as if he couldn't comprehend—then, as he does, a look of shocked indignation comes over his face*) No! What do you think I am, Pa? I never would! She's not that kind! Why, I—I love her! I'm going to marry her—after I get out of college! She's said she would! We're engaged!

MILLER (*with great relief*) All right. That's all I wanted to know. We won't talk any more about it. (*He gives him an approving pat on the back.*)

RICHARD I don't see how you could think— Did that old idiot McComber say that about me?

MILLER (*joking now*) Shouldn't call your future father-in-law names, should you? 'Tain't respectful. (*Then after a glance at* RICHARD's *indignant face—points to the slips of paper on the table*) Well, you can't exactly blame old Dave, can you, when you read through that literature you wished on his innocent daughter?

RICHARD (*sees the slips for the first time and is overcome by embarrassment, which he immediately tries to cover up with a superior carelessness*) Oh, so that's why. He found those, did he? I told her to be careful—Well, it'll do him good to read the truth about life for once and get rid of his old-fogy ideas.

MILLER I'm afraid I've got to agree with him, though, that they're hardly fit reading for a young girl. (*Then with subtle flattery*) They're all well enough, in their way, for you who're a man, but— Think it over, and see if you don't agree with me.

RICHARD (*embarrassedly*) Aw, I only did it because I liked them—and I wanted her to face life as it is. She's so darned afraid of life—afraid of her Old Man—afraid of people saying this or that about her—afraid of being in love—afraid of everything. She's even afraid to let me kiss her. I thought, maybe, reading those things —they're beautiful, aren't they, Pa?—I thought they would give her the spunk to lead her own life, and not be—always thinking of being afraid.

MILLER I see. Well, I'm afraid she's still afraid. (*He takes the letter from the table.*) Here's a letter from her he said to give you. (RICHARD *takes the letter from him uncertainly, his expression changing to one of apprehension.* MILLER *adds with a kindly smile*) You better be prepared for a bit of a blow. But never mind. There's lots of other fish in the sea. (RICHARD *is not listening to him, but staring at the letter with a sort of fascinated dread.* MILLER *looks into his son's face a second, then turns away, troubled and embarrassed.)* Darn it! I better go upstairs and get rigged out or I never will get to that picnic. *(He moves awkwardly and self consciously off through the front parlor.* RICHARD *continues to stare at the letter for a moment—then girds up his courage and tears it open and begins to read swiftly. As he reads his face grows more and more wounded and tragic, until at the end his mouth draws down at the corners, as if he were about to break into tears. With an effort he forces them back and his face grows flushed with humiliation and wronged anger.)*

RICHARD *(blurts out to himself)* The little coward! I hate her! She can't treat me like that! I'll show her! *(At the sound of voices from the front parlor, he quickly shoves the letter into the inside pocket of his coat and does his best to appear calm and indifferent, even attempting to whistle "Waiting at the Church." But the whistle peters out miserably as his mother,* LILY, *and* SID *enter from the front parlor. They are dressed in all the elaborate paraphernalia of motoring at that period—linen dusters, veils, goggles,* SID *in a snappy cap.)*

MRS. MILLER Well, we're about ready to start at last, thank goodness! Let's hope no more callers are on the way. What did that McComber want, Richard, do you know? Sid couldn't tell us.

RICHARD You can search me. Ask Pa.

MRS. MILLER *(immediately sensing something "down" in his manner—going to him worriedly)* Why, whatever's the matter with you, Richard? You sound as if you'd lost your last friend! What is it?

RICHARD *(desperately)* I—I don't feel so well—my stomach's sick.

MRS. MILLER *(immediately all sympathy—smoothing his hair back from his forehead)* You poor boy! What a shame—on the Fourth, too, of all days! *(Turning to the others)* Maybe I better stay home with him, if he's sick.

LILY Yes, I'll stay, too.

RICHARD (*more desperately*) No! You go, Ma! I'm not really sick. I'll be all right. You go. I want to be alone! (*Then, as a louder bang comes from in back as* TOMMY *sets off a cannon cracker, he jumps to his feet.*) Darn Tommy and his darned firecrackers! You can't get any peace in this house with that darned kid around! Darn the Fourth of July, anyway! I wish we still belonged to England! (*He strides off in an indignant fury of misery through the front parlor.*)

MRS. MILLER (*stares after him worriedly—then sighs philosophically*) Well, I guess he can't be so very sick—after that. (*She shakes her head.*) He's a queer boy. Sometimes I can't make head or tail of him.

MILLER (*calls from the front door beyond the back parlor*) Come along folks. Let's get started.

SID We're coming, Nat. (*He and the two women move off through the front parlor.*)

Curtain

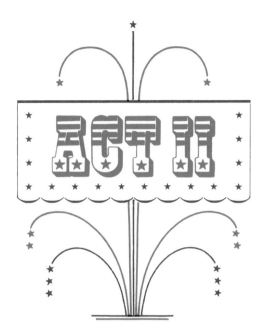

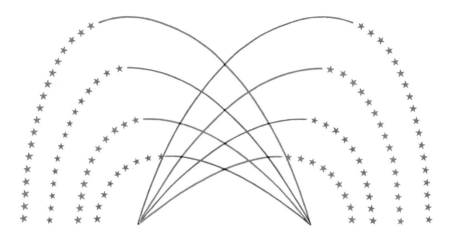

DINING-ROOM *of the* MILLER *home—a little after 6 o'clock in the evening of the same day.*

The room is much too small for the medium-priced, formidable dining-room set, especially now when all the leaves of the table are in. At left, toward rear, is a double doorway with sliding doors and portières leading into the back parlor. In the rear wall, left, is the door to the pantry. At the right of door is the china closet with its display of the family cut glass and fancy china. In the right wall are two windows looking out on a side lawn. In front of the windows is a heavy, ugly sideboard with three pieces of old silver on its top. In the left wall, extreme front, is a screen door opening on a side porch. A dark rug covers most of the floor. The table, with a chair at each end, left and right, three chairs on the far side, facing front, and two on the near side, their backs to front, takes up most of the available space. The walls are papered in a somber brown and dark-red design.

MRS. MILLER *is supervising and helping the Second Girl,* NORAH, *in the setting of the table.* NORAH *is a clumsy, heavy-handed, heavy-footed, long-jawed, beamingly good-natured young Irish girl—a "greenhorn."*

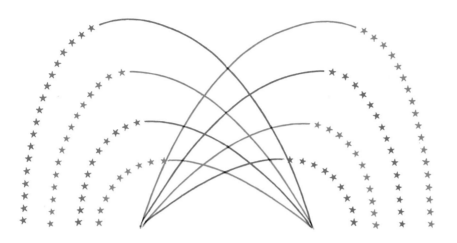

MRS. MILLER   I really think you better put on the lights, Norah. It's getting so cloudy out, and this pesky room is so dark, anyway.

NORAH   Yes, Mum. (*She stretches awkwardly over the table to reach the chandelier that is suspended from the middle of the ceiling and manages to turn one light on—scornfully*) Arrah, the contraption!

MRS. MILLER   (*worriedly*) Careful!

NORAH   Careful as can be, Mum. (*But in moving around to reach the next bulb she jars heavily against the table.*)

MRS. MILLER   There! I knew it! I do wish you'd watch—!

NORAH   (*a flustered appeal in her voice*) Arrah, what have I done wrong now?

MRS. MILLER   (*draws a deep breath—then sighs helplessly*) Oh, nothing. Never mind the rest of the lights. You might as well go out in the kitchen and wait until I ring.

NORAH   (*relieved and cheerful again*) Yes, Mum. (*She starts for the pantry.*)

MRS. MILLER   But there's one thing— (NORAH *turns apprehensively.*) No, two things—things I've told you over and over, but you always forget. Don't pass the plates on the wrong side at dinner tonight, and do be careful not to let that pantry door slam behind you. Now you will try to remember, won't you?

NORAH Yes, Mum. (*She goes into the pantry and shuts the door behind her with exaggerated care as* MRS. MILLER *watches her apprehensively.* MRS. MILLER *sighs and reaches up with difficulty and turns on another of the four lights in the chandelier. As she is doing so,* LILY *enters from the back parlor.*)

LILY Here, let me do that, Essie. I'm taller. You'll only strain yourself. (*She quickly lights the other two bulbs.*)

MRS. MILLER (*gratefully*) Thank you, Lily. It's a stretch for me, I'm getting so fat.

LILY But where's Norah? Why didn't she—?

MRS. MILLER (*exasperatedly*) Oh, that girl! Don't talk about her! She'll be the death of me! She's that thick, you honestly wouldn't believe it possible.

LILY (*smiling*) Why, what did she do now?

MRS. MILLER Oh, nothing. She means all right.

LILY Anything else I can do, Essie?

MRS. MILLER Well, she's got the table all wrong. We'll have to reset it. But you're always helping me. It isn't fair to ask you—in your vacation. You need your rest after teaching a pack of wild Indians of kids all year.

LILY (*beginning to help with the table*) You know I love to help. It makes me feel I'm some use in this house instead of just sponging—

MRS. MILLER (*indignantly*) Sponging! You pay, don't you?

LILY   Almost nothing. And you and Nat only take that little to make me feel better about living with you. (*Forcing a smile*) I don't see how you stand me—having a cranky old maid around all the time.

MRS. MILLER   What nonsense you talk! As if Nat and I weren't only too tickled to death to have you! Lily Miller, I've no patience with you when you go on like that. We've been over this a thousand times before, and still you go on! Crazy, that's what it is! (*She changes the subject abruptly.*) What time's it getting to be?

LILY   (*looking at her watch*) Quarter past six.

MRS. MILLER   I do hope those men folks aren't going to be late for dinner. (*She sighs.*) But I suppose with that darned Sachem Club picnic it's more likely than not. (LILY *looks worried, and sighs.* MRS. MILLER *gives her a quick side glance.*) I see you've got your new dress on.

LILY   (*embarrassedly*) Yes, I thought—if Sid's taking me to the fire-works—I ought to spruce up a little.

MRS. MILLER   (*looking away*) Hmm. (*A pause—then she says with an effort to be casual*) You mustn't mind if Sid comes home feeling a bit—gay. I expect Nat to—and we'll have to listen to all those old stories of his about when he was a boy. You know what those picnics are, and Sid'd be running into all his old friends.

LILY   (*agitatedly*) I don't think he will—this time—not after his promise.

MRS. MILLER   (*avoiding looking at her*) I know. But men are weak. (*Then quickly*) That was a good notion of Nat's, getting Sid the job on the Waterbury *Standard*. All he ever needed was to get away from the rut he was in here. He's the kind that's the victim of his friends. He's easily led—but there's no real harm in him, you know that. (LILY *keeps silent, her eyes downcast.* MRS. MILLER *goes on meaningly*) He's making good money in Waterbury, too—thirty-five a week. He's in a better position to get married than he ever was.

LILY (*stiffly*) Well, I hope he finds a woman who's willing—though after he's through with his betting on horse races, and dice, and playing Kelly pool, there won't be much left for a wife—even if there was nothing else he spent his money on.

MRS. MILLER Oh, he'd give up all that—for the right woman. (*Suddenly she comes directly to the point.*) Lily, why don't you change your mind and marry Sid and reform him? You love him and always have—

LILY (*stiffly*) I can't love a man who drinks.

MRS. MILLER You can't fool me. I know darned well you love him. And he loves you and always has.

LILY Never enough to stop drinking for. (*Cutting off* MRS. MILLER'S *reply*) No, it's no good in your talking, Essie. We've been over this a thousand times before and I'll always feel the same as long as Sid's the same. If he gave me proof he'd—but even then I don't believe I could. It's sixteen years since I broke off our engagement, but what made me break it off is as clear to me today as it was then. It was what he'd be liable to do now to anyone who married him—his taking up with bad women.

MRS. MILLER (*protests half-heartedly*) But he's always sworn he got raked into that party and never had anything to do with those harlots.

LILY Well, I don't believe him—didn't then and don't now. I do believe he didn't deliberately plan to, but—Oh, it's no good talking, Essie. What's done is done. But you know how much I like Sid—in spite of everything. I know he was just born to be what he is—irresponsible, never meaning to harm but harming in spite

of himself. But don't talk to me about marrying him—because I never could.

MRS. MILLER (*angrily*) He's a dumb fool—a stupid dumb fool, that's what he is!

LILY (*quietly*) No. He's just Sid.

MRS. MILLER It's a shame for you—a measly shame—you that would have made such a wonderful wife for any man—that ought to have your own home and children!

LILY (*winces but puts her arm around her affectionately—gently*) Now don't you go feeling sorry for me. I won't have that. Here I am, thanks to your and Nat's kindness, with the best home in the world; and as for the children, I feel the same love for yours as if they were mine, and I didn't have the pain of bearing them. And then there are all the boys and girls I teach every year. I like to feel I'm a sort of second mother to them and helping them to grow up to be good men and women. So I don't feel such a useless old maid, after all.

MRS. MILLER (*kisses her impulsively—her voice husky*) You're a good woman, Lily—too good for the rest of us. (*She turns away, wiping a tear furtively—then abruptly changing the subject*) Good gracious, if I'm not forgetting one of the most important things! I've got to warn that Tommy against giving me away to Nat about the fish. He knows, because I had to send him to market for it, and he's liable to burst out laughing—

LILY Laughing about what?

MRS. MILLER (*guiltily*) Well, I've never told you, because it seemed sort of a sneaking trick, but you know how Nat carries on about not being able to eat bluefish.

LILY I know he says there's a certain oil in it that poisons him.

MRS. MILLER (*chuckling*) Poisons him, nothing! He's been eating bluefish for years—only I tell him each time it's weakfish. We're having it tonight—and I've got to warn that young imp to keep his face straight.

LILY (*laughing*) Aren't you ashamed, Essie!

MRS. MILLER Not much, I'm not! I like bluefish! (*She laughs.*) Where is Tommy? In the sitting-room?

LILY No, Richard's there alone. I think Tommy's out on the piazza with Mildred. (MRS. MILLER *bustles out through the back parlor. As soon as she is gone, the smile fades from* LILY's *lips. Her face grows sad and she again glances nervously at her watch.* RICHARD *appears from the back parlor, moving in an aimless way. His face wears a set expression of bitter gloom; he exudes tragedy. For* RICHARD, *after his first outburst of grief and humiliation, has begun to take a masochistic satisfaction in his great sorrow, especially in the concern which it arouses in the family circle. On seeing his aunt, he gives her a dark look and turns and is about to stalk back toward the sitting-room when she speaks to him pityingly.*) Feel any better, Richard?

RICHARD (*somberly*) I'm all right, Aunt Lily. You mustn't worry about me.

LILY (*going to him*) But I do worry about you. I hate to see you so upset.

RICHARD It doesn't matter. Nothing matters.

LILY (*puts her arm around him sympathetically*) You really mustn't let yourself take it so seriously. You know, something happens and things like that come up, and we think there's no hope—

RICHARD   Things like what come up?

LILY   What's happened between you and Muriel.

RICHARD   (*with disdain*) Oh, her! I wasn't even thinking about her. I was thinking about life.

LILY   But then—if we really, *really* love—why, then something else is bound to happen soon that changes everything again, and it's all as it was before the misunderstanding, and everything works out all right in the end. That's the way it is with life.

RICHARD   (*with a tragic sneer*) Life! Life is a joke! And everything comes out all wrong in the end!

LILY   (*a little shocked*) You mustn't talk that way. But I know you don't mean it.

RICHARD   I do too mean it! You can have your silly optimism, if you like, Aunt Lily. But don't ask me to be so blind. I'm a pessimist! (*Then with an air of cruel cynicism*) As for Muriel, that's all dead and past. I was only kidding her, anyway, just to have a little fun, and she took it seriously, like a fool. (*He forces a cruel smile to his lips.*) You know what they say about women and trolley cars, Aunt Lily: there's always another one along in a minute.

LILY   (*really shocked this time*) I don't like you when you say such horrible, cynical things. It isn't nice.

RICHARD   Nice! that's all you women think of! I'm proud to be a cynic. It's the only thing you can be when you really face life. I suppose you think I ought to be heartbroken about Muriel—a little coward that's afraid to say her soul's her own, and keeps tied to her father's apron strings! Well, not for mine! There's plenty of other fish in the sea! (*As he is finishing, his mother comes back through the back parlor.*)

MRS. MILLER Why, hello. You here, Richard? Getting hungry, I suppose?

RICHARD (*indignantly*) I'm not hungry a bit! That's all you think of, Ma—food!

MRS. MILLER Well, I must say I've never noticed you to hang back at meal times. (*To* LILY) What's that he was saying about fish in the sea?

LILY (*smiling*) He says he's through with Muriel now.

MRS. MILLER (*tartly—giving her son a rebuking look*) She's through with him, he means! The idea of your sending a nice girl like her things out of those indecent books! (*Deeply offended,* RICHARD *disdains to reply but stalks woundedly to the screen door at left, front, and puts a hand on the knob.*) Where are you going?

RICHARD (*quotes from "Candida" in a hollow voice*) "Out, then, into the night with me!" (*He stalks out, slamming the door behind him.*)

MRS. MILLER (*calls*) Well, don't you go far, 'cause dinner'll be ready in a minute, and I'm not coming running after you! (*She turns to* LILY *with a chuckle.*) Goodness, that boy! He ought to be on the stage! (*She mimics*) "Out—into the night"—and it isn't even dark yet! He got that out of one of those books, I suppose. Do you know, I'm actually grateful to old Dave McComber for putting an end to his nonsense with Muriel. I never did approve of Richard getting so interested in girls. He's not old enough for such silliness. Why, seems to me it was only yesterday he was still a baby. (*She sighs—then matter-of-factly*) Well, nothing to do now till those men turn up. No use standing here like gawks. We might as well go in the sitting-room and be comfortable.

LILY (*the nervous, worried note in her voice again*) Yes, we might as well. (*They go out through the back parlor. They have no sooner disappeared than the screen door is opened cautiously and* RICHARD *comes back in the room.*)

RICHARD (*stands inside the door, looking after them—quotes bitterly*) "They do not know the secret in the poet's heart." (*He comes nearer the table and surveys it, especially the cut-glass dish containing olives, with contempt and mutters disdainfully*) Food! (*But the dish of olives seems to fascinate him and presently he has approached nearer, and stealthily lifts a couple and crams them into his mouth. He is just reaching out for more when the pantry door is opened slightly and* NORAH *peers in.*)

NORAH Mister Dick, you thief, lave them olives alone, or the missus'll be swearing it was me at them!

RICHARD (*draws back his hand as if he had been stung—too flustered to be anything but guilty boy for a second*) I—I wasn't eating—

NORAH Oho, no, of course not, divil fear you, you was only feeling their pulse! (*Then warningly*) Mind what I'm saying now, or I'll have to tell on you to protect me good name! (*She draws back into the pantry, closing the door.* RICHARD *stands, a prey to feelings of bitterest humiliation and seething revolt against everyone and everything. A low whistle comes from just outside the porch door. He starts. Then a masculine voice calls: "Hey, Dick." He goes over to the screen door grumpily—then as he recognizes the owner of the voice, his own as he answers becomes respectful and admiring.*)

RICHARD Oh, hello, Wint. Come on in. (*He opens the door and* WINT SELBY *enters and stands just inside the door.* SELBY *is nineteen, a classmate of* ARTHUR's *at Yale. He's a typical, good-looking college boy of the period, not the athletic but the hell-raising sport type. He is tall, blond, dressed in extreme collegiate cut.*)

WINT (*as he enters—warningly, in a low tone*) Keep it quiet, Kid. I don't want the folks to know I'm here. Tell Art I want to see him a second—on the Q.T.

RICHARD Can't. He's up at the Rands'—won't be home before ten, anyway.

WINT (*irritably*) Damn, I thought he'd be here for dinner. (*More irritably*) Hell, that gums the works for fair!

RICHARD (*ingratiatingly*) What is it, Wint? Can't I help?

WINT (*gives him an appraising glance*) I might tell you, if you can keep your face shut.

RICHARD I can.

WINT Well, I ran into a couple of swift babies from New Haven this after, and I dated them up for tonight, thinking I could catch Art. But now it's too late to get anyone else and I'll have to pass it up. I'm nearly broke and I can't afford to blow them both to drinks.

RICHARD (*with shy eagerness*) I've got eleven dollars saved up. I could loan you some.

WINT (*surveys him appreciatively*) Say, you're a good sport. (*Then shaking his head*) Nix, Kid, I don't want to borrow your money. (*Then getting an idea*) But say, have you got anything on for tonight?

RICHARD No.

WINT Want to come along with me? (*Then quickly*) I'm not trying to lead you astray, understand. But it'll be a help if you would just sit around with Belle and feed her a few drinks while I'm off with Edith. (*He winks.*) See what I mean? You don't have to do anything, not even take a glass of beer—unless you want to.

RICHARD (*boastfully*) Aw, what do you think I am—a rube?

WINT You mean you're game for anything that's doing?

RICHARD Sure I am!

WINT Ever been out with any girls—I mean, real swift ones that there's something doing with, not these dead Janes around here?

RICHARD (*lies boldly*) Aw, what do you think? Sure I have!

WINT Ever drink anything besides sodas?

RICHARD Sure. Lots of times. Beer and sloe-gin fizz and—Manhattans.

WINT (*impressed*) Hell, you know more than I thought. (*Then considering*) Can you fix it so your folks won't get wise? I don't want your old man coming after me. You can get back half-past ten or eleven, though, all right. Think you can cook up some lie to cover that? (*As* RICHARD *hesitates—encouraging him*) Ought to be easy—on the Fourth.

RICHARD Sure. Don't worry about that.

WINT But you've got to keep your face closed about this, you hear?—to Art and everybody else. I tell you straight, I wouldn't ask you to come if I wasn't in a hole—and if I didn't know you were coming down to Yale next year, and didn't think you're giving me the straight goods about having been around before. I don't want to lead you astray.

RICHARD (*scornfully*) Aw, I told you that was silly.

WINT Well, you be at the Pleasant Beach House at half-past nine then. Come in the back room. And don't forget to grab some cloves to take the booze off your breath.

RICHARD Aw, I know what to do.

WINT See you later, then. (*He starts out and is just about to close the door when he thinks of something.*) And say, I'll say you're a

Harvard freshman, and you back me up. They don't know a damn thing about Harvard. I don't want them thinking I'm travelling around with any high-school kid.

RICHARD Sure. That's easy.

WINT So long, then. You better beat it right after your dinner while you've got a chance, and hang around until it's time. Watch your step, Kid.

RICHARD So long. (*The door closes behind* WINT. RICHARD *stands for a moment, a look of bitter, defiant rebellion coming over his face, and mutters to himself*) I'll show her she can't treat me the way she's done! I'll show them all! (*Then the front door is heard slamming, and a moment later* TOMMY *rushes in from the back parlor.*)

TOMMY Where's Ma?

RICHARD (*surlily*) In the sitting-room. Where did you think, Bonehead?

TOMMY Pa and Uncle Sid are coming. Mid and I saw them from the front piazza. Gee, I'm glad. I'm awful hungry, ain't you? (*He rushes out through the back parlor, calling*) Ma! They're coming! Let's have dinner quick! (*A moment later* MRS. MILLER *appears from the back parlor accompanied by* TOMMY, *who keeps insisting urgently*) Gee, but I'm awful hungry, Ma!

MRS. MILLER I know. You always are. You've got a tapeworm, that's what I think.

TOMMY Have we got lobsters, Ma? Gee, I love lobsters.

MRS. MILLER Yes, we've got lobsters. And fish. You remember what I told you about that fish. (*He snickers.*) Now, do be quiet, Tommy! (*Then with a teasing smile at* RICHARD) Well, I'm glad to see you've got back out of the night, Richard. (*He scowls and turns* his back on her. LILY *appears through the back parlor, nervous and apprehensive. As she does so, from the front yard* SID's *voice is heard singing "Poor John!"* MRS. MILLER *shakes her head forebodingly—but, so great is the comic spell for her even in her brother's voice, a humorous smile hovers at the corners of her lips.)* Mmm! Mmm! Lily, I'm afraid—

LILY (*bitterly*) Yes, I might have known. (MILDRED *runs in through the back parlor. She is laughing to herself a bit shamefacedly. She rushes to her mother.*)

MILDRED Ma, Uncle Sid's— (*She whispers in her ear.*)

MRS. MILLER Never mind! You shouldn't notice such things—at your age! And don't you encourage him by laughing at his foolishness, you hear!

TOMMY You needn't whisper, Mid. Think I don't know? Uncle Sid's soused again.

MRS. MILLER (*shakes him by the arm indignantly*) You be quiet! Did I ever! You're getting too smart! (*Gives him a push.*) Go to your place and sit right down and not another word out of you!

TOMMY (*aggrieved—rubbing his arm as he goes to his place*) Aw, Ma!

MRS. MILLER And you sit down, Richard and Mildred. You better, too, Lily. We'll get him right in here and get some food in him. He'll be all right then. (RICHARD, *preserving the pose of the bitter, disillusioned pessimist, sits down in his place in the chair at right of the two whose backs face front.* MILDRED *takes the other chair facing back, at his left.* TOMMY *has already slid into the end chair at right of those at the rear of table facing front.* LILY *sits in the one of those at left, by the head of the table, leaving the middle one*

[SID's] *vacant. While they are doing this, the front screen door is heard slamming and* NAT's *and* SID's *laughing voices, raised as they come in and for a moment after, then suddenly cautiously lowered.* MRS. MILLER *goes to the entrance to the back parlor and calls peremptorily)* You come right in here! Don't stop to wash up or anything. Dinner's coming right on the table.

MILLER's VOICE (*jovially*) All right, Essie. Here we are! Here we are!

MRS. MILLER (*goes to pantry door, opens it and calls*) All right, Norah. You can bring in the soup. (*She comes back to the back-parlor entrance just as* MILLER *enters. He isn't drunk by any means. He is just mellow and benignly ripened. His face is one large, smiling, happy beam of utter appreciation of life. All's right with the world, so satisfyingly right that he becomes sentimentally moved even to think of it.*)

MILLER Here we are, Essie! Right on the dot! Here we are! (*He pulls her to him and gives her a smacking kiss on the ear as she jerks her head away.* MILDRED *and* TOMMY *giggle.* RICHARD *holds rigidly aloof and disdainful, his brooding gaze fixed on his plate.* LILY *forces a smile.*)

MRS. MILLER (*pulling away—embarrassedly, almost blushing*) Don't, you Crazy! (*Then recovering herself—tartly*) So I see, you're here! And if I didn't, you've told me four times already!

MILLER (*beamingly*) Now, Essie, don't be critical. Don't be carpingly critical. Good news can stand repeating, can't it? 'Course it can! (*He slaps her jovially on her fat buttocks.* TOMMY *and* MILDRED *roar with glee. And* NORAH, *who has just entered from the pantry with a huge tureen of soup in her hands, almost drops it as she explodes in a merry guffaw.*)

MRS. MILLER (*scandalized*) Nat! Aren't you ashamed!

MILLER   Couldn't resist it! Just simply couldn't resist it! (NORAH, *still standing with the soup tureen held out stiffly in front of her, again guffaws.*)

MRS. MILLER   (*turns on her with outraged indignation*) Norah! Bring that soup here this minute! (*She stalks with stiff dignity toward her place at the foot of the table, right.*)

NORAH   (*guiltily*) Yes, Mum. (*She brings the soup around the head of the table, passing* MILLER.)

MILLER   (*jovially*) Why, hello, Norah!

MRS. MILLER   Nat! (*She sits down stiffly at the foot of the table.*)

NORAH   (*rebuking him familiarly*) Arrah now, don't be making me laugh and getting me into trouble!

MRS. MILLER   Norah!

NORAH   (*a bit resentfully*) Yes, Mum. Here I am. (*She sets the soup tureen down with a thud in front of* MRS. MILLER *and passes around the other side, squeezing with difficulty between the china closet and the backs of chairs at the rear of the table.*)

MRS. MILLER   Tommy! Stop spinning your napkin ring! How often have I got to tell you? Mildred! Sit up straight in your chair! Do you want to grow up a humpback? Richard! Take your elbows off the table!

MILLER   (*coming to his place at the head of the table, rubbing his hands together genially*) Well, well, well. Well, well, well. It's good to be home again. (NORAH *exits into the pantry and lets the door slam with a bang behind her.*)

MRS. MILLER   (*jumps*) Oh! (*Then exasperatedly*) Nat, I do wish you wouldn't encourage that stupid girl by talking to her, when I'm doing my best to train—

MILLER (*beamingly*) All right, Essie. Your word is law! (*Then laughingly*) We did have the darndest fun today! And Sid was the life of that picnic! You ought to have heard him! Honestly, he had that crowd just rolling on the ground and splitting their sides! He ought to be on the stage.

MRS. MILLER (*as* NORAH *comes back with a dish of saltines—begins ladling soup into the stack of plates before her*) He ought to be at this table eating something to sober him up, that's what he ought to be! (*She calls*) Sid! You come right in here! (*Then to* NORAH, *handing her a soup plate*) Here, Norah. (NORAH *begins passing soup.*) Sit down, Nat, for goodness sakes. Start eating, everybody. Don't wait for me. You know I've given up soup.

MILLER (*sits down but bends forward to call to his wife in a confidential tone*) Essie—Sid's sort of embarrassed about coming—I mean I'm afraid he's a little bit—not too much, you understand—but he met such a lot of friends and—well, you know, don't be hard on him. Fourth of July is like Christmas—comes but once a year. Don't pretend to notice, eh? And don't you kids, you hear! And don't you, Lily. He's scared of you.

LILY (*with stiff meekness*) Very well, Nat.

MILLER (*beaming again—calls*) All right, Sid. The coast's clear. (*He begins to absorb his soup ravenously.*) Good soup, Essie! Good soup! (*A moment later* SID *makes his entrance from the back parlor. He is in a condition that can best be described as blurry. His movements have a hazy uncertainty about them. His shiny fat face is one broad, blurred, puckish, naughty-boy grin; his eyes have a blurred, wondering vagueness. As he enters he makes a solemnly intense effort to appear casual and dead, cold sober. He waves his hand aimlessly and speaks with a silly gravity.*)

SID Good evening. (*They all answer "Good evening," their eyes on their plates. He makes his way vaguely toward his place, continuing his grave effort at conversation*) Beautiful evening. I never remember seeing—more beautiful sunset. (*He bumps vaguely into* LILY's *chair as he attempts to pass behind her—immediately he is all grave politeness.*) Sorry—sorry, Lily—deeply sorry.

LILY (*her eyes on her plate—stiffly*) It's all right.

SID (*manages to get into his chair at last—mutters to himself*) Wha' was I sayin'? Oh, sunsets. But why butt in? Hasn't sun—perfect right to set? Mind y'r own business. (*He pauses thoughtfully, considering this—then looks around from face to face, fixing each with a vague, blurred, wondering look, as if some deep puzzle were confronting him. Then suddenly he grins mistily and nods with satisfaction.*) And there you are! Am I right?

MILLER (*humoring him*) Right.

SID Right! (*He is silent, studying his soup plate, as if it were some strange enigma. Finally he looks up and regards his sister and asks with wondering amazement*) Soup?

MRS. MILLER Of course, it's soup. What did you think it was? And you hurry up and eat it.

SID (*again regards his soup with astonishment*) Well! (*Then suddenly*) Well, all right then! Soup be it! (*He picks up his spoon and begins to eat, but after two tries in which he finds it difficult to locate his mouth, he addresses the spoon plaintively*) Spoon, is this any way to treat a pal? (*Then suddenly comically angry, putting the spoon down with a bang*) Down with spoons! (*He raises his soup plate and declaims*) "We'll drink to the dead already, and hurrah for the next who dies." (*Bowing solemnly to right and left*) Your good health, ladies and gents. (*He starts drinking the soup.*

MILLER *guffaws and* MILDRED *and* TOMMY *giggle. Even* RICHARD *forgets his melancholy and snickers, and* MRS. MILLER *conceals a smile. Only* LILY *remains stiff and silent.*)

MRS. MILLER   (*with forced severity*) Sid!

SID   (*peers at her muzzily, lowering the soup plate a little from his lips*) Eh?

MRS. MILLER   Oh, nothing, Never mind.

SID   (*solemnly offended*) Are you—publicly rebuking me before assembled—? Isn't soup liquid? Aren't liquids drunk? (*Then considering this to himself*) What if they are drunk? It's a good man's failing. (*He again peers mistily about at the company.*) Am I right or wrong?

MRS. MILLER   Hurry up and finish your soup, and stop talking nonsense!

SID   (*turning to her—again offendedly*) Oh, no, Essie, if I ever so far forget myself as to drink a leg of lamb, then you might have some—excuse for— Just think of waste effort eating soup with spoons—fifty gruelling lifts per plate—billions of soup-eaters on globe—why, it's simply staggering! (*Then darkly to himself*) No more spoons for me! If I want to develop my biceps, I'll buy Sandow Exerciser! (*He drinks the rest of his soup in a gulp and beams around at the company, suddenly all happiness again.*) Am I right, folks?

MILLER   (*who has been choking with laughter*) Haw, haw! You're right, Sid.

SID   (*peers at him blurredly and shakes his head sadly*) Poor old Nat! Always wrong—but heart of gold, heart of purest gold. And drunk again, I regret to note. Sister, my heart bleeds for you and your poor fatherless chicks!

MRS. MILLER   *(restraining a giggle—severely)* Sid! Do shut up for a minute! Pass me your soup plates, everybody. If we wait for that girl to take them, we'll be here all night. *(They all pass their plates, which* MRS. MILLER *stacks up and then puts on the sideboard. As she is doing this,* NORAH *appears from the pantry with a platter of broiled fish. She is just about to place this before* MILLER *when* SID *catches her eye mistily and rises to his feet, making her a deep, uncertain bow.)*

SID   *(raptly)* Ah, Sight for Sore Eyes, my beautiful Macushla, my star-eyed Mavourneen—

MRS. MILLER   Sid!

NORAH   *(immensely pleased—gives him an arch, flirtatious glance)* Ah sure, Mister Sid, it's you that have kissed the Blarney Stone, when you've a drop taken!

MRS. MILLER   *(outraged)* Norah! Put down that fish!

NORAH   *(flusteredly)* Yes, Mum. *(She attempts to put the fish down hastily before* MILLER, *but her eyes are fixed nervously on* MRS. MILLER *and she gives* MILLER *a nasty swipe on the side of the head with the edge of the dish.)*

MILLER   Ouch! *(The children, even* RICHARD, *explode into laughter.)*

NORAH   *(almost lets the dish fall)* Oh, glory be to God! It is hurted you are?

MILLER   *(rubbing his head—good-naturedly)* No, no harm done. Only careful, Norah, careful.

NORAH   *(gratefully)* Yes, sorr. *(She thumps down the dish in front of him with a sigh of relief.)*

SID   *(who is still standing—with drunken gravity)* Careful, Mavourneen, careful! You might have hit him some place besides the head. Always aim at his head, remember—so as not to worry us. (*Again the children explode. Also* NORAH. *Even* LILY *suddenly lets out an hysterical giggle and is furious with herself for doing so.*)

LILY I'm so sorry, Nat. I didn't mean to laugh. (*Turning on* SID *furiously*) Will you please sit down and stop making a fool of yourself? (SID *gives her a hurt, mournful look and then sinks meekly down on his chair.*)

NORAH (*grinning cheerfully, gives* LILY *a reassuring pat on the back*) Ah, Miss Lily, don't mind him. He's only under the influence. Sure, there's no harm in him at all.

MRS. MILLER Norah! (NORAH *exits hastily into the pantry, letting the door slam with a crash behind her. There is silence for a moment as* MILLER *serves the fish and it is passed around.* NORAH *comes back with the vegetables and disappears again, and these are dished out.*)

MILLER (*is about to take his first bite—stops suddenly and asks his wife*) This isn't, by any chance, bluefish, is it, my dear?

MRS. MILLER (*with a warning glance at* TOMMY) Of course not. You know we never have bluefish, on account of you.

MILLER (*addressing the table now with the gravity of a man confessing his strange peculiarities*) Yes, I regret to say, there's a certain peculiar oil in bluefish that invariably poisons me. (*At this,* TOMMY *cannot stand it any more but explodes into laughter.* MRS. MILLER, *after a helpless glance at him, follows suit; then* LILY *goes off into uncontrollable, hysterical laughter, and* RICHARD *and* MILDRED *are caught in the contagion.* MILLER *looks around at them with a weak smile, his dignity now ruffled a bit.*) Well, I must say I don't see what's so darned funny about my being poisoned.

SID (*peers around him—then with drunken cunning*) Aha! Nat, I suspect—plot! This fish looks blue to me—very blue—in fact despondent, desperate, and— (*He points his fork dramatically at* MRS. MILLER.) See how guilty she looks a ver—veritable Lucretia Georgia! Can it be this woman has been slowly poisoning you all these years? And how well—you've stood it! What an iron constitution! Even now, when you are invariably at death's door, I can't believe— (*Everyone goes off into uncontrollable laughter.*)

MILLER (*grumpily*) Oh, give us a rest, you darned fool! A joke's a joke, but— (*He addresses his wife in a wounded tone*) Is this true, Essie?

MRS. MILLER (*wiping the tears from her eyes—defiantly*) Yes, it is true, if you must know, and you'd never have suspected it, if it weren't for that darned Tommy, and Sid poking his nose in. You've eaten bluefish for years and thrived on it and it's all nonsense about that peculiar oil.

MILLER (*deeply offended*) Kindly allow me to know my own constitution! Now I think of it, I've felt upset afterwards every damned time we've had fish! (*He pushes his plate away from him with proud renunciation.*) I can't eat this.

MRS. MILLER (*insultingly matter-of-fact*) Well, don't then. There's lots of lobster coming and you can fill up on that. (RICHARD *suddenly bursts out laughing again.*)

MILLER (*turns to him caustically*) You seem in a merry mood, Richard. I thought you were the original of the Heart Bowed Down today.

SID (*with mock condolence*) Never mind, Dick. Let them—scoff! What can they understand about girls whose hair sizzchels, whose lips are fireworks, whose eyes are red-hot sparks—

MILDRED (*laughing*) Is that what he wrote to Muriel? (*Turning to her brother*) You silly goat, you!

RICHARD (*surlily*) Aw, shut up, Mid. What do I care about her? I'll show all of you how much I care!

MRS. MILLER Pass your plates as soon as you're through, everybody. I've rung for the lobster. And that's all. You don't get any dessert or tea after lobster, you know. (NORAH *appears bearing a platter of cold boiled lobsters which she sets before* MILLER, *and disappears.*)

TOMMY Gee, I love lobster! (MILLER *puts one on each plate, and they are passed around and everyone starts in pulling the cracked shells apart.*)

MILLER (*feeling more cheerful after a couple of mouthfuls—determining to give the conversation another turn, says to his daughter*) Have a good time at the beach, Mildred?

MILDRED Oh, fine, Pa, thanks. The water was wonderful and warm.

MILLER Swim far?

MILDRED Yes, for me. But that isn't so awful far.

MILLER Well, you ought to be a good swimmer, if you take after me. I used to be a regular water rat when I was a boy. I'll have to go down to the beach with you one of these days—though I'd be rusty, not having been in in all these years. (*The reminiscent look comes into his eyes of one about to embark on an oft-told tale of childhood adventure.*) You know, speaking of swimming, I never go down to that beach but what it calls to mind the day I and Red Sisk went in swimming there and I saved his life. (*By this time the family are beginning to exchange amused, guilty glances. They all know what is coming.*)

SID (*with a sly, blurry wink around*) Ha! Now we—have it again!

MILLER (*turning on him*) Have what?

SID Nothing—go on with your swimming—don't mind me.

MILLER (*glares at him—but immediately is overcome by the reminiscent mood again*) Red Sisk—his father kept a blacksmith shop where the Union Market is now—we kids called him Red because he had the darndest reddest crop of hair—

SID (*as if he were talking to his plate*) Remarkable!—the curious imagination—of little children.

MRS. MILLER (*as she sees* MILLER *about to explode—interposes tactfully*) Sid! Eat your lobster and shut up! Go on, Nat.

MILLER (*gives* SID *a withering look—then is off again*) Well, as I was saying, Red and I went swimming that day. Must have been—let me see—Red was fourteen, bigger and older than me, I was only twelve—forty-five years ago—wasn't a single house down there then—but there was a stake out where the whistling buoy is now, about a mile out. (TOMMY, *who has been having difficulty restraining himself, lets out a stifled giggle.* MILLER *bends a frowning gaze on him.*) One more sound out of you, young man, and you'll leave the table!

MRS. MILLER (*quickly interposing, trying to stave off the story*) Do eat your lobster, Nat. You didn't have any fish, you know.

MILLER (*not liking the reminder—pettishly*) Well, if I'm going to be interrupted every second anyway— (*He turns to his lobster and chews in silence for a moment.*)

MRS. MILLER (*trying to switch the subject*) How's Anne's mother's rheumatism, Mildred?

MILDRED Oh, she's much better, Ma. She was in wading today. She says salt water's the only thing that really helps her bunion.

MRS. MILLER Mildred! Where are your manners? At the table's no place to speak of—

MILLER *(fallen into the reminiscent obsession again)* Well, as I was saying, there was I and Red, and he dared me to race him out to the stake and back. Well, I didn't let anyone dare me in those days. I was a spunky kid. So I said all right and we started out. We swam and swam and were pretty evenly matched; though, as I've said, he was bigger and older than me, but finally I drew ahead. I was going along easy, with lots in reserve, not a bit tired, when suddenly I heard a sort of gasp from behind me—like this—"Help." *(He imitates. Everyone's eyes are firmly fixed on his plate, except* SID'S.) And I turned and there was Red, his face all pinched and white, and he says weakly: "Help, Nat! I got a cramp in my leg!" Well, I don't mind telling you I got mighty scared. I didn't know what to do. Then suddenly I thought of the pile. If I could pull him to that, I could hang on to him till someone'd notice us. But the pile was still—well, I calculate it must have been two hundred feet away.

SID Two hundred and fifty!

MILLER *(in confusion)* What's that?

SID Two hundred *and* fifty! I've taken down the distance every time you've saved Red's life for thirty years and the mean average to that pile is two hundred and fifty feet! *(There is a burst of laughter from around the table.* SID *continues complainingly)* Why didn't you let that Red drown, anyway, Nat? I never knew him but I know I'd never have liked him.

MILLER *(really hurt, forces a feeble smile to his lips and pretends to be a good sport about it)* Well, guess you're right, Sid. Guess I have told that one too many times and bored everyone. But it's a good true story for kids because it illustrates the danger of being foolhardy in the water—

MRS. MILLER *(sensing the hurt in his tone, comes to his rescue)* Of course it's a good story—and you tell it whenever you've a mind to. And you, Sid, if you were in any responsible state, I'd give you a good piece of my mind for teasing Nat like that.

MILLER *(with a sad, self-pitying smile at his wife)* Getting old, I guess, Mother—getting to repeat myself. Someone ought to stop me.

MRS. MILLER No such thing! You're as young as you ever were. *(She turns on* SID *again angrily.)* You eat your lobster and maybe it'll keep your mouth shut!

SID *(after a few chews—irrepressibly)* Lobster! Did you know, Tommy, your Uncle Sid is the man invented lobster? Fact! One day—when I was building the Pyramids—took a day off and just dashed off lobster. He was bigger 'n' older than me and he had the darndest reddest crop of hair but I dashed him off just the same! Am I right, Nat? *(Then suddenly in the tones of a side-show barker)* Ladies *and* Gents—

MRS. MILLER Mercy sakes! Can't you shut up?

SID In this cage you see the lobster. You will not believe me, ladies *and* gents, but it's a fact that this interesting bivalve only makes love to his mate once in every thousand years—but, dearie me, how he does enjoy it! *(The children roar.* LILY *and* MRS. MILLER *laugh in spite of themselves—then look embarrassed.* MILLER *guffaws—then suddenly grows shocked.)*

MILLER Careful, Sid, careful. Remember you're at home.

TOMMY *(suddenly in a hoarse whisper to his mother, with an awed glance of admiration at his uncle)* Ma! Look at him! He's eating that claw, shells and all!

MRS. MILLER *(horrified)* Sid, do you want to kill yourself? Take it away from him, Lily!

SID (*with great dignity*) But I prefer the shells. All famous epicures prefer the shells—to the less delicate, coarser meat. It's the same with clams. Unless I eat the shells there is a certain, peculiar oil that invariably poisons— Am I right, Nat?

MILLER (*good-naturedly*) You seem to be getting a lot of fun kidding me. Go ahead, then. I don't mind.

MRS. MILLER He better go right up to bed for a while, that's what he better do.

SID (*considering this owlishly*) Bed? Yes, maybe you're right. (*He gets to his feet.*) I am not at all well—in very delicate condition—we are praying for a boy. Am I right, Nat? Nat, I kept telling you all day I was in delicate condition and yet you kept forcing demon chowder on me, although you knew full well—even if you were full—that there is a certain, peculiar oil in chowder that invariably— (*They are again all laughing—*LILY, *hysterically.*)

MRS. MILLER *Will* you get to bed, you idiot!

SID (*mutters graciously*) Immediately—if not sooner. (*He turns to pass behind* LILY, *then stops, staring down at her.*) But wait. There is still a duty I must perform. No day is complete without it. Lily, answer once and for all, will you marry me?

LILY (*with an hysterical giggle*) No, I won't—never!

SID (*nodding his head*) Right! And perhaps it's all for the best. For how could I forget the pre-precepts taught me at mother's dying knee. "Sidney," she said, "never marry a woman who drinks! Lips that touch liquor shall never touch yours!" (*Gazing at her mournfully*) Too bad! So fine a woman once—and now such a slave to rum! (*Turning to* NAT) What can we do to save her, Nat? (*In a hoarse, confidential whisper*) Better put her in institution where she'll be removed from temptation! The mere smell of it seems to drive her frantic!

MRS. MILLER (*struggling with her laughter*) You leave Lily alone, and go to bed!

SID Right! (*He comes around behind* LILY'*s chair and moves toward the entrance to the back parlor—then suddenly turns and says with a bow*) Good night, ladies—and gents. We will meet—bye and bye! (*He gives an imitation of a Salvation Army drum*) Boom! Boom! Boom! Come and be saved, Brothers! (*He starts to sing the old Army hymn*)

> "In the sweet
> Bye and bye
> We will meet on that beautiful shore."

(*He turns and marches solemnly out through the back parlor, singing*)

> "Work and pray
> While you may.
> We will meet in the sky bye and bye."

(MILLER *and his wife and the children are all roaring with laughter.* LILY *giggles hysterically.*)

MILLER (*subsiding at last*) Haw, haw. He's a case, if ever there was one! Darned if you can help laughing at him—even when he's poking fun at you!

MRS. MILLER Goodness, but he's a caution! Oh, my sides ache, I declare! I was trying so hard not to—but you can't help it, he's so silly! But I suppose we really shouldn't. It only encourages him. But, my lands—!

LILY (*suddenly gets up from her chair and stands rigidly, her face working—jerkily*) That's just it—you shouldn't—even I laughed—it does encourage—that's been his downfall—everyone always laughing, everyone always saying what a card he is, what a case, what a caution, so funny—and he's gone on—and we're all responsible—making it easy for him—we're all to blame—and all we do is laugh!

MILLER (*worriedly*) Now, Lily, now, you mustn't take on so. It isn't as serious as all that.

LILY (*bitterly*) Maybe—it is—to me. Or was—once. (*Then contritely*) I'm sorry, Nat. I'm sorry, Essie. I didn't mean to—I'm not feeling myself tonight. If you'll excuse me, I'll go in the front parlor and lie down on the sofa a while.

MRS. MILLER Of course, Lily. You do whatever you've a mind to. (LILY *goes out.*)

MILLER (*frowning—a little shamefaced*) Hmm. I suppose she's right. Never knew Lily to come out with things that way before. Anything special happened, Essie?

MRS. MILLER Nothing I know—except he'd promised to take her to the fireworks.

MILLER That's so. Well, supposing I take her? I don't want her to feel disappointed.

MRS. MILLER (*shaking her head*) Wild horses couldn't drag her there now.

MILLER Hmm. I thought she'd got completely over her foolishness about him long ago.

MRS. MILLER She never will.

MILLER She'd better. He's got fired out of that Waterbury job—told me at the picnic after he'd got enough Dutch courage in him.

MRS. MILLER Oh, dear! Isn't he the fool!

MILLER I knew something was wrong when he came home. Well, I'll find a place for him on my paper again, of course. He always was the best news-getter this town ever had. But I'll tell him he's got to stop his damn nonsense.

MRS. MILLER *(doubtfully)* Yes.

MILLER Well, no use sitting here mourning over spilt milk. (*He gets up, and* RICHARD, MILDRED, TOMMY *and* MRS. MILLER *follow his example, the children quiet and a bit awed.*) You kids go out in the yard and try to keep quiet for a while, so's your Uncle Sid'll get to sleep and your Aunt Lily can rest.

TOMMY *(mournfully)* Ain't we going to set off the skyrockets and Roman candles, Pa?

MILLER Later, Son, later. It isn't dark enough for them yet anyway.

MILDRED Come on, Tommy. I'll see he keeps quiet, Pa.

MILLER That's a good girl. (MILDRED *and* TOMMY *go out through the screen door.* RICHARD *remains standing, sunk in bitter, gloomy thoughts.* MILLER *glances at him—then irritably*) Well, Melancholy Dane, what are you doing?

RICHARD *(darkly)* I'm going out—for a while. (*Then suddenly*) Do you know what I think? It's Aunt Lily's fault, Uncle Sid's going to ruin. It's all because he loves her, and she keeps him dangling after her, and eggs him on and ruins his life—like all women love to ruin men's lives! I don't blame him for drinking himself to death! What does he care if he dies, after the way she's treated him! I'd do the same thing myself if I were in his boots!

MRS. MILLER *(indignantly)* Richard! You stop that talk!

RICHARD *(quotes bitterly)*

"Drink! for you know not whence you come nor why.
Drink! for you know not why you go nor where!"

MILLER (*losing his temper—harshly*) Listen here, young man! I've had about all I can stand of your nonsense for one day! You're growing a lot too big for your size, seems to me! You keep that damn fool talk to yourself, you hear me—or you're going to regret it! Mind now! (*He strides angrily away through the back parlor.*)

MRS. MILLER (*still indignant*) Richard, I'm ashamed of you, that's what I am. (*She follows her husband.* RICHARD *stands for a second, bitter, humiliated, wronged, even his father turned enemy, his face growing more and more rebellious. Then he forces a scornful smile to his lips.*)

RICHARD Aw, what the hell do I care? I'll show them! (*He turns and goes out the screen door.*)

Curtain

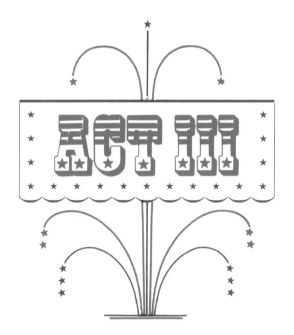

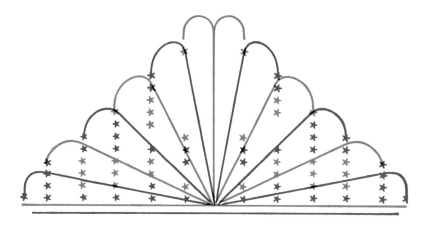

Scene I

THE BACK ROOM *of a bar in a small hotel—a small, dingy room, dimly lighted by two fly-specked globes in a fly-specked gilt chandelier suspended from the middle of the ceiling. At left, front, is the swinging door leading to the bar. At rear of door, against the wall, is a nickel-in-the-slot player-piano. In the rear wall, right, is a door leading to the "Family Entrance" and the stairway to the upstairs rooms. In the middle of the right wall is a window with closed shutters. Three tables with stained tops, four chairs around each table, are placed at center, front, at right, toward rear, and at rear, center. A brass cuspidor is on the floor by each table. The floor is unswept, littered with cigarette and cigar butts. The hideous saffron-colored wall-paper is blotched and spotted.*

It is about 10 o'clock the same night. RICHARD *and* BELLE *are discovered sitting at the table at center,* BELLE *at left of it,* RICHARD *in the next chair at the middle of table, rear, facing front.*

BELLE *is twenty, a rather pretty peroxide blonde, a typical college "tart" of the period, and of the cheaper variety, dressed with tawdry flashiness. But she is a fairly recent recruit to the ranks, and is still a bit remorseful behind her make-up and defiantly careless manner.*

BELLE *has an empty gin-rickey glass before her,* RICHARD *a half-empty glass of beer. He looks horribly timid, embarrassed and guilty, but at the same time thrilled and proud of at last mingling with the pace that kills.*

The player-piano is grinding out "Bedelia." The BARTENDER, *a stocky young Irishman with a foxily cunning, stupid face and a cynically wise grin, stands just inside the bar entrance, watching them over the swinging door.*

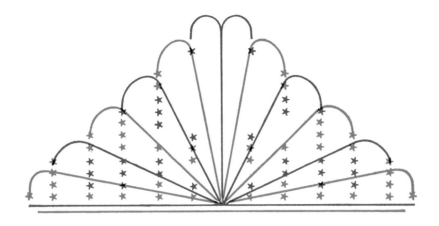

BELLE (*with an impatient glance at her escort—rattling the ice in her empty glass*) Drink up your beer, why don't you? It's getting flat.

RICHARD (*embarrassedly*) I let it get that way on purpose. I like it better when it's flat. (*But he hastily gulps down the rest of his glass, as if it were some nasty-tasting medicine. The* BARTENDER *chuckles audibly.* BELLE *glances at him.*)

BELLE (*nodding at the player-piano scornfully*) Say, George, is "Bedelia" the latest to hit this hick burg? Well, it's only a couple of years old! You'll catch up in time! Why don't you get a new roll for that old box?

BARTENDER (*with a grin*) Complain to the boss, not me. We're not used to having Candy Kiddoes like you around—or maybe we'd get up to date.

BELLE (*with a professionally arch grin at him*) Don't kid me, please. I can't bear it. (*Then she sings to the music from the piano, her eyes now on* RICHARD.) "Bedelia, I'd like to feel yer." (*The* BARTENDER *laughs. She smirks at* RICHARD.) Ever hear those words to it, Kid?

RICHARD (*who has heard them but is shocked at hearing a girl say them—putting on a blasé air*) Sure, lots of times. That's old.

BELLE   (*edging her chair closer and putting a hand over one of his*) Then why don't you act as if you knew what they were all about?

RICHARD   (*terribly flustered*) Sure, I've heard that old parody lots of times. What do you think I am?

BELLE   I don't know, Kid. Honest to God, you've got me guessing.

BARTENDER   (*with a mocking chuckle*) He's a hot sport, can't you tell it? I never seen such a spender. My head's dizzy bringing you in drinks!

BELLE   (*laughs irritably—to* RICHARD) Don't let him kid you. You show him. Loosen up and buy another drink, what say?

RICHARD   (*humiliated—manfully*) Sure. Excuse me. I was thinking of something else. Have anything you like. (*He turns to the BAR-TENDER who has entered from the bar*) See what the lady will have —and have one on me yourself.

BARTENDER   (*coming to the table—with a wink at* BELLE) That's talking! Didn't I say you were a sport? I'll take a cigar on you. (*To* BELLE) What's yours, Kiddo—the same?

BELLE   Yes. And forget the house rules this time and remember a rickey is supposed to have gin in it.

BARTENDER   (*grinning*) I'll try to—seeing it's you. (*Then to* RICHARD) What's yours—another beer?

RICHARD   (*shyly*) A small one, please. I'm not thirsty.

BELLE   (*calculatedly taunting*) Say, honest, are things that slow up at Harvard? If they had you down at New Haven, they'd put you in a kindergarten! Don't be such a dead one! Filling up on beer will only make you sleepy. Have a man's drink!

RICHARD   (*shamefacedly*) All right. I was going to. Bring me a sloe-gin fizz.

BELLE (*to* BARTENDER) And make it a real one.

BARTENDER (*with a wink*) I get you. Something that'll warm him up, eh? (*He goes into the bar, chuckling.*)

BELLE (*looks around the room—irritably*) Christ, what a dump! (RICH-ARD *is startled and shocked by this curse and looks down at the table.*) If this isn't the deadest burg I ever struck! Bet they take the sidewalks in after nine o'clock! (*Then turning on him*) Say, honestly, Kid, does your mother know you're out?

RICHARD (*defensively*) Aw, cut it out, why don't you—trying to kid me!

BELLE (*glances at him—then resolves on a new tack—patting his hand*) All right. I didn't mean to, Dearie. Please don't get sore at me.

RICHARD I'm not sore.

BELLE (*seductively*) You see, it's this way with me. I think you're one of the sweetest kids I've ever met—and I could like you such a lot if you'd give me half a chance—instead of acting so cold and in-different.

RICHARD I'm not cold and indifferent. (*Then solemnly tragic*) It's only that I've got—a weight on my mind.

BELLE (*impatiently*) Well, get if off your mind and give something else a chance to work. (*The* BARTENDER *comes in, bringing the drinks.*)

BARTENDER (*setting them down—with a wink at* BELLE) This'll warm him for you. Forty cents, that is—with the cigar.

RICHARD (*pulls out his roll and hands a dollar bill over—with exaggerated carelessness*) Keep the change. (BELLE *emits a gasp and seems about to protest, then thinks better of it. The* BARTENDER *cannot believe his luck for a moment—then pockets the bill hastily, as if afraid* RICHARD *will change his mind.*)

BARTENDER (*respect in his voice*) Thank you, sir.

RICHARD (*grandly*) Don't mention it.

BARTENDER I hope you like the drink. I took special pains with it. (*The voice of the* SALESMAN, *who has just come in the bar, calls* "Hey! Anybody here?" *and a coin is rapped on the bar.*) I'm coming. (*The* BARTENDER *goes out.*)

BELLE (*remonstrating gently, a new appreciation for her escort's possibilities in her voice*) You shouldn't be so generous, Dearie. Gets him in bad habits. A dime would have been plenty.

RICHARD Ah, that's all right. I'm no tightwad.

BELLE That's the talk I like to hear. (*With a quick look toward the bar, she stealthily pulls up her dress—to* RICHARD's *shocked fascination—and takes a package of cheap cigarettes from her stocking.*) Keep an eye out for that bartender, Kid, and tell me if you see him coming. Girls are only allowed to smoke upstairs in the rooms, he said.

RICHARD (*embarrassedly*) All right. I'll watch.

BELLE (*having lighted her cigarette and inhaled deeply, holds the package out to him*) Have a Sweet? You smoke, don't you?

RICHARD (*taking one*) Sure! I've been smoking for the last two years—on the sly. But next year I'll be allowed—that is, pipes and cigars. (*He lights his cigarette with elaborate nonchalance, puffs, but does not inhale—then, watching her, with shocked concern*) Say, you oughtn't to inhale like that! Smoking's awful bad for girls, anyway, even if they don't—

BELLE (*cynically amused*) Afraid it will stunt my growth? Gee, Kid, you are a scream! You'll grow up to be a minister yet! (RICHARD *looks shamefaced. She scans him impatiently—then holds up her*

drink.) Well, here's how! Bottoms up, now! Show me you really know how to drink. It'll take that load off your mind. (RICHARD *follows her example and they both drink the whole contents of their glasses before setting them down.*) There! That's something like! Feel better?

RICHARD (*proud of himself—with a shy smile*) You bet.

BELLE Well, you'll feel still better in a minute—and then maybe you won't be so distant and unfriendly, eh?

RICHARD I'm not.

BELLE Yes, you are. I think you just don't like me.

RICHARD (*more manfully*) I do too like you.

BELLE How much? A lot?

RICHARD Yes, a lot.

BELLE Show me how much! (*Then as he fidgets embarrassedly*) Want me to come sit on your lap?

RICHARD Yes—I—(*She comes and sits on his lap. He looks desperately uncomfortable, but the gin is rising to his head and he feels proud of himself and devilish, too.*)

BELLE Why don't you put your arm around me? (*He does so awkwardly.*) No, not that dead way. Hold me tight. You needn't be afraid of hurting me. I like to be held tight, don't you?

RICHARD Sure I do.

BELLE 'Specially when it's by a nice handsome kid like you. (*Ruffling his hair*) Gee, you've got pretty hair, do you know it? Honest, I'm awfully strong for you! Why can't you be about me? I'm not so awfully ugly, am I?

RICHARD No, you're—you're pretty.

BELLE   You don't say it as if you meant it.

RICHARD   I do mean it—honest.

BELLE   Then why don't you kiss me? (*She bends down her lips toward his. He hesitates, then kisses her and at once shrinks back.*) Call that kissing? Here. (*She holds his head and fastens her lips on his and holds them there. He starts and struggles. She laughs.*) What's the matter, Honey Boy? Haven't you ever kissed like that before?

RICHARD   Sure. Lots of times.

BELLE   Then why did you jump as if I'd bitten you? (*Squirming around on his lap*) Gee, I'm getting just crazy about you! What shall we do about it, eh? Tell me.

RICHARD   I—don't know. (*Then boldly*) I—I'm crazy about you, too.

BELLE   (*kissing him again*) Just think of the wonderful time Edith and your friend, Wint, are having upstairs—while we sit down here like two dead ones. A room only costs two dollars. And, seeing I like you so much, I'd only take five dollars—from you. I'd do it for nothing—for you—only I've got to live and I owe my room rent in New Haven—and you know how it is. I get ten dollars from everyone else. Honest! (*She kisses him again, then gets up from his lap—briskly*) Come on. Go out and tell the bartender you want a room. And hurry. Honest, I'm so strong for you I can hardly wait to get you upstairs!

RICHARD   (*starts automatically for the door to the bar—then hesitates, a great struggle going on in his mind—timidity, disgust at the money element, shocked modesty, and the guilty thought of* MURIEL, *fighting it out with the growing tipsiness that makes him want to be a hell of a fellow and go in for all forbidden fruit, and makes this tart a romantic, evil vampire in his eyes. Finally, he stops and mutters in confusion*) I can't.

BELLE   What, are you too bashful to ask for a room? Let me do it, then. (*She starts for the door.*)

RICHARD   (*desperately*) No—I don't want you to—I don't want to.

BELLE   (*surveying him, anger coming into her eyes*) Well, if you aren't the lousiest cheap skate!

RICHARD   I'm not a cheap skate!

BELLE   Keep me around here all night fooling with you when I might be out with some real live one—if there is such a thing in this burg! —and now you quit on me! Don't be such a piker! You've got five dollars! I seen it when you paid for the drinks, so don't hand me any lies!

RICHARD   I— Who said I hadn't? And I'm not a piker. If you need the five dollars so bad—for your room rent—you can have it without—I mean, I'll be glad to give— (*He has been fumbling in his pocket and pulls out his nine-dollar roll and holds out the five to her.*)

BELLE   (*hardly able to believe her eyes, almost snatches it from his hand— then laughs and immediately becomes sentimentally grateful*) Thanks, Kid. Gee—oh, thanks—Gee, forgive me for losing my temper and bawling you out, will you? Gee, you're a regular peach! You're the nicest kid I've ever met! (*She kisses him and he grins proudly, a hero to himself now on many counts.*) Gee, you're a peach! Thanks, again!

RICHARD   (*grandly—and quite tipsily*) It's—nothing—only too glad. (*Then boldly*) Here—give me another kiss, and that'll pay me back.

BELLE   (*kissing him*) I'll give you a thousand, if you want 'em. Come on, let's sit down, and we'll have another drink—and this time I'll blow you just to show my appreciation. (*She calls*) Hey, George! bring us another round—the same!

RICHARD (*a remnant of caution coming to him*) I don't know as I ought to—

BELLE Oh, another won't hurt you. And I want to blow you, see. (*They sit down in their former places.*)

RICHARD (*boldly draws his chair closer and puts an arm around her—tipsily*) I like you a lot—now I'm getting to know you. You're a darned nice girl.

BELLE Nice is good! Tell me another! Well, if I'm so nice, why didn't you want to take me upstairs? That's what I don't get.

RICHARD (*lying boldly*) I did want to—only I— (*Then he adds solemnly*) I've sworn off. (*The* BARTENDER *enters with the drinks.*)

BARTENDER (*setting them on the table*) Here's your pleasure. (*Then regarding* RICHARD's *arm about her waist*) Ho-ho, we're coming on, I see. (RICHARD *grins at him muzzily.*)

BELLE (*digs into her stocking and gives him a dollar*) Here. This is mine. (*He gives her change and she tips him a dime, and he goes out. She puts the five* RICHARD *had given her in her stocking and picks up her glass.*) Here's how—and thanks again. (*She sips.*)

RICHARD (*boisterously*) Bottoms up! Bottoms up! (*He drinks all of his down and sighs with exaggerated satisfaction.*) Gee, that's good stuff, all right. (*Hugging her*) Give me another kiss, Belle.

BELLE (*kisses him*) What did you mean a minute ago when you said you'd sworn off?

RICHARD (*solemnly*) I took an oath I'd be faithful.

BELLE (*bristling*) I'm not good enough to talk about her, I suppose?

RICHARD I didn't—mean that. You're all right. (*Then with tipsy gravity*) Only you oughtn't to lead this kind of life. It isn't right—for a nice girl like you. Why don't you reform?

BELLE (*sharply*) Nix on that line of talk! Can it, you hear! You can do a lot with me for five dollars—but you can't reform me, see. Mind your own business, Kid, and don't butt in where you're not wanted!

RICHARD I—I didn't mean to hurt your feelings.

BELLE I know you didn't mean. You're only like a lot of people who mean well, to hear them tell it. (*Changing the subject*) So you're faithful to your one love, eh? (*With an ugly sneer*) And how about her? Bet you she's out with a guy under some bush this minute, giving him all he wants. Don't be a sucker, Kid! Even the little flies do it!

RICHARD (*starting up from his chair again—angrily*) Don't you say that! Don't you dare!

BELLE (*unimpressed—with a cynical shrug of her shoulders*) All right. Have it your own way and be a sucker! It cuts no ice with me.

RICHARD You don't know her or—

BELLE And don't want to. Shut up about her, can't you? (*She stares before her bitterly.* RICHARD *subsides into scowling gloom. He is becoming perceptibly more intoxicated with each moment now. The* BARTENDER *and the* SALESMAN *appear just inside the swinging door. The* BARTENDER *nods toward* BELLE, *giving the* SALESMAN *a wink. The* SALESMAN *grins and comes into the room, carrying his highball in his hand. He is a stout, jowly-faced man in his late thirties, dressed with cheap nattiness, with the professional breeziness and jocular, kid-'em-along manner of his kind.* BELLE *looks up as he enters and he and she exchange a glance of complete recognition. She knows his type by heart and he knows hers.*)

SALESMAN (*passes by her to the table at right—grinning genially*) Good evening.

BELLE Good evening.

SALESMAN (*sitting down*) Hope I'm not butting in on your party—but my dogs were giving out standing at that bar.

BELLE All right with me. (*Giving* RICHARD *a rather contemptuous look*) I've got no party on.

SALESMAN That sounds hopeful.

RICHARD (*suddenly recites sentimentally*)

> "But I wouldn't do such, 'cause I loved her too much,
> But I learned about women from her."

(*Turns to scowl at the* SALESMAN—*then to* BELLE) Let's have 'nother drink!

BELLE You've had enough. (RICHARD *subsides, muttering to himself.*)

SALESMAN What is it—a child poet or a child actor?

BELLE Don't know. Got me guessing.

SALESMAN Well, if you could shake the cradle-robbing act, maybe we could do a little business.

BELLE That's easy. I just pull my freight. (*She shakes* RICHARD *by the arm.*) Listen, Kid. Here's an old friend of mine, Mr. Smith of New Haven, just come in. I'm going over and sit at his table for a while, see. And you better go home.

RICHARD (*blinking at her and scowling*) I'm never going home! I'll show them!

BELLE Have it your own way—only let me up. (*She takes his arm from around her and goes to sit by the* SALESMAN. RICHARD *stares after her offendedly.*)

RICHARD Go on. What do I care what you do? (*He recites scornfully*)

"For a woman's only a woman, but a good cigar's a smoke."

SALESMAN (*as* BELLE *sits beside him*) Well, what kind of beer will you have, Sister?

BELLE Mine's a gin rickey.

SALESMAN You've got extravagant tastes, I'm sorry to see.

RICHARD (*begins to recite sepulchrally*)

> "Yet each man kills the thing he loves,
> By each let this be heard."

SALESMAN (*grinning*) Say, this is rich! (*He calls encouragement.*) That's swell dope, young feller. Give us some more.

RICHARD (*ignoring him—goes on more rhetorically*)

> "Some do it with a bitter look,
> Some with a flattering word,
> The coward does it with a kiss,
> The brave man with a sword!"

(*He stares at* BELLE *gloomily and mutters tragically*) I did it with a kiss! I'm a coward.

SALESMAN That's the old stuff, Kid. You've got something on the ball, all right, all right! Give us another—right over the old pan, now!

BELLE (*with a laugh*) Get the hook!

RICHARD (*glowering at her—tragically*)

> "'Oho,' they cried, 'the world is wide,
> But fettered limbs go lame!
> And once, or twice, to throw the dice
> Is a gentlemanly game,
> But he does not win who plays with Sin
> In the secret House of Shame!'"

BELLE (*angrily*) Aw, can it! Give us a rest from that bunk!

SALESMAN (*mockingly*) This gal of yours don't appreciate poetry. She's a lowbrow. But I'm the kid that eats it up. My middle name is Kelly and Sheets! Give us some more of the same! Do you know "The Lobster and the Wise Guy"? (*Turns to* BELLE *seriously*) No kidding, that's a peacherino. I heard a guy recite it at Poli's. Maybe this nut knows it. Do you, Kid? (*But* RICHARD *only glowers at him gloomily without answering.*)

BELLE (*surveying* RICHARD *contemptuously*) He's copped a fine skinful— and gee, he's hardly had anything.

RICHARD (*suddenly—with a dire emphasis*) "And then—at ten o'clock— Eilert Lovborg will come—with vine leaves in his hair!"

BELLE And bats in his belfry, if he's you!

RICHARD (*regards her bitterly—then starts to his feet bellicosely—to the* SALESMAN) I don't believe you ever knew her in New Haven at all! You just picked her up now! You leave her alone, you hear! You won't do anything to her—not while I'm here to protect her!

BELLE (*laughing*) Oh, my God! Listen to it!

SALESMAN Ssshh! This is a scream! Wait! (*He addresses* RICHARD *in tones of exaggerated melodrama*) Curse you, Jack Dalton, if I won't un- hand her, what then?

RICHARD (*threateningly*) I'll give you a good punch in the snoot, that's what! (*He moves toward their table.*)

SALESMAN (*with mock terror—screams in falsetto*) Help! Help! (*The* BAR- TENDER *comes in irritably.*)

BARTENDER Hey! Cut out the noise. What the hell's up with you?

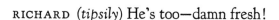

RICHARD *(tipsily)* He's too—damn fresh!

SALESMAN *(with a wink)* He's going to murder me. *(Then gets a bright idea for eliminating* RICHARD—*seriously to the* BARTENDER*)* It's none of my business, Brother, but if I were in your boots I'd give this young souse the gate. He's under age; any fool can see that.

BARTENDER *(guiltily)* He told me he was over eighteen.

SALESMAN Yes, and I tell you I'm the Pope—but you don't have to believe me. If you're not looking for trouble, I'd advise you to get him started for some other gin mill and let them do the lying, if anything comes up.

BARTENDER Hmm. *(He turns to* RICHARD *angrily and gives him a push.)* Come on, now. On your way! You'll start no trouble in here! Beat it now!

RICHARD I will not beat it!

BARTENDER Oho, won't you? *(He gives him another push that almost sends him sprawling.)*

BELLE *(callously)* Give him the bum's rush! I'm sick of his bull! *(*RICHARD *turns furiously and tries to punch the* BARTENDER.*)*

BARTENDER *(avoids the punch)* Oho, you would, would you! *(He grabs* RICHARD *by the back of the neck and the seat of the pants and marches him ignominiously toward the swinging door.)*

RICHARD Leggo of me, you dirty coward!

BARTENDER Quiet now—or I'll pin a Mary Ann on your jaw that'll quiet you! *(He rushes him through the screen door and a moment later the outer doors are heard swinging back and forth.)*

SALESMAN *(with a chuckle)* Hand it to me, Kid. How was that for a slick way of getting rid of him?

BELLE (*suddenly sentimental*) Poor kid. I hope he makes home all right. I liked him—before he got soused.

SALESMAN Who is he?

BELLE The boy who's upstairs with my friend told me, but I didn't pay much attention. Name's Miller. His old man runs a paper in this one-horse burg, I think he said.

SALESMAN (*with a whistle*) Phew! He must be Nat Miller's kid, then.

BARTENDER (*coming back from the bar*) Well, he's on his way—with a good boot in the tail to help him!

SALESMAN (*with a malicious chuckle*) Yes? Well, maybe that boot will cost you a job, Brother. Know Nat Miller who runs the *Globe?* That's his kid.

BARTENDER (*his face falling*) The hell he is! Who said so?

SALESMAN This baby doll. (*Getting up*) Say, I'll go keep cases on him—see he gets on the trolley all right, anyway. Nat Miller's a good scout. (*He hurries out.*)

BARTENDER (*viciously*) God damn the luck! If he ever finds out I served his kid, he'll run me out of town. (*He turns on* BELLE *furiously*) Why didn't you put me wise, you lousy tramp, you!

BELLE Hey! I don't stand for that kind of talk—not from no hick beer-squirter like you, see!

BARTENDER (*furiously*) You don't, don't you? Who was it but you told me to hand him dynamite in that fizz? (*He gives her chair a push that almost throws her to the floor.*) Beat it, you—and beat it quick—or I'll call Sullivan from the corner and have you run in for street-walking! (*He gives her a push that lands her against the family entrance door.*) Get the hell out of here—and no long waits!

BELLE *(opens the door and goes out—turns and calls back viciously)* I'll fix you for this, you thick Mick, if I have to go to jail for it. *(She goes out and slams the door.)*

BARTENDER *(looks after her worriedly for a second—then shrugs his shoulders)* That's only her bull. *(Then with a sigh as he returns to the bar)* Them lousy tramps is always getting this dump in Dutch!

Curtain

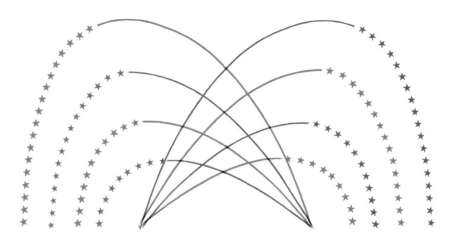

Scene II

SAME AS ACT ONE—*sitting-room of the Miller home—about* 11 *o'clock the same night.*

MILLER *is sitting in his favorite rocking-chair at left of table, front. He has discarded collar and tie, coat and shoes, and wears an old, worn, brown dressing-gown and disreputable-looking carpet slippers. He has his reading specs on and is running over items in a newspaper. But his mind is plainly preoccupied and worried, and he is not paying much attention to what he reads.*

MRS. MILLER *sits by the table at right, front. She also has on her specs. A sewing basket is on her lap and she is trying hard to keep her attention fixed on the doily she is doing. But, as in the case of her husband, but much more apparently, her mind is preoccupied, and she is obviously on tenterhooks of nervous uneasiness.*

LILY *is sitting in the armchair by the table at rear, facing right. She is pretending to read a novel, but her attention wanders, too, and her expression is sad, although now it has lost all its bitterness and become submissive and resigned again.*

MILDRED *sits at the desk at right, front, writing two words over and over again, stopping each time to survey the result critically, biting her tongue, intensely concentrated on her work.*

TOMMY *sits on the sofa at left, front. He has had a hard day and is terribly sleepy but will not acknowledge it. His eyes blink shut on him, his head begins to nod, but he isn't giving up, and every time he senses any of the family glancing in his direction, he goads himself into a bright-eyed wakefulness.*

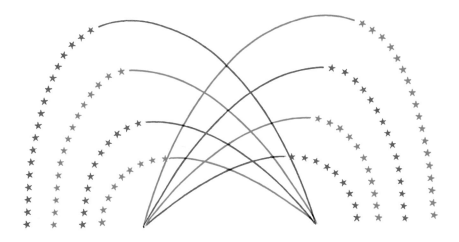

MILDRED (*finally surveys the two words she has been writing and is satisfied with them*) There. (*She takes the paper over to her mother.*) Look, Ma. I've been practising a new way of writing my name. Don't look at the others, only the last one. Don't you think it's the real goods?

MRS. MILLER (*pulled out of her preoccupation*) Don't talk that horrible slang. It's bad enough for boys, but for a young girl supposed to have manners—my goodness, when I was your age, if my mother'd ever heard me—

MILDRED Well, don't you think it's nice, then?

MRS. MILLER (*sinks back into preoccupation—scanning the paper—vaguely*) Yes, very nice, Mildred—very nice, indeed. (*Hands the paper back mechanically.*)

MILDRED (*is a little piqued, but smiles*) Absent-minded! I don't believe you even saw it. (*She passes around the table to show her AUNT LILY. MILLER gives an uneasy glance at his wife and then, as if afraid of meeting her eye, looks quickly back at his paper again.*)

MRS. MILLER (*staring before her—sighs worriedly*) Oh, I do wish Richard would come home!

MILLER   There now, Essie. He'll be in any minute now. Don't you worry about him.

MRS. MILLER   But I do worry about him!

LILY   (*surveying* MILDRED's *handiwork—smiling*) This is fine, Mildred. Your penmanship is improving wonderfully. But don't you think that maybe you've got a little too many flourishes?

MILDRED   (*disappointedly*) But, Aunt Lily, that's just what I was practising hardest on.

MRS. MILLER   (*with another sigh*) What time is it now, Nat?

MILLER   (*adopting a joking tone*) I'm going to buy a clock for in here. You have me reaching for my watch every couple of minutes. (*He has pulled his watch out of his vest pocket—with forced carelessness*) Only a little past ten.

MRS. MILLER   Why, you said it was that an hour ago! Nat Miller, you're telling me a fib, so's not to worry me. You let me see that watch!

MILLER   (*guiltily*) Well, it's quarter to eleven—but that's not so late—when you remember it's Fourth of July.

MRS. MILLER   If you don't stop talking Fourth of July—! To hear you go on, you'd think that was an excuse for anything from murder to picking pockets!

MILDRED   (*has brought her paper around to her father and now shoves it under his nose*) Look, Pa.

MILLER   (*seizes on this interruption with relief*) Let's see. Hmm. Seems to me you've been inventing a new signature every week lately. What are you in training for—writing checks? You must be planning to catch a rich husband.

MILDRED   (*with an arch toss of her head*) No wedding bells for me! But how do you like it, Pa?

MILLER   It's overpowering—no other word for it, overpowering! You could put it on the Declaration of Independence and not feel ashamed.

MRS. MILLER   (*desolately, almost on the verge of tears*) It's all right for you to laugh and joke with Mildred! I'm the only one in this house seems to care— (*Her lips tremble.*)

MILDRED   (*a bit disgustedly*) Ah, Ma, Dick only sneaked off to the fireworks at the beach, you wait and see.

MRS. MILLER   Those fireworks were over long ago. If he had, he'd be home.

LILY   (*soothingly*) He probably couldn't get a seat, the trolleys are so jammed, and he had to walk home.

MILLER   (*seizing on this with relief*) Yes, I never thought of that, but I'll bet that's it.

MILDRED   Ah, don't let him worry you, Ma. He just wants to show off he's heartbroken about that silly Muriel—and get everyone fussing over him and wondering if he hasn't drowned himself or something.

MRS. MILLER   (*snappily*) You be quiet! The way you talk at times, I really believe you're that hard-hearted you haven't got a heart in you! (*With an accusing glance at her husband*) One thing I know, you don't get that from me! (*He meets her eye and avoids it guiltily. She sniffs and looks away from him around the room.* TOMMY, *who is nodding and blinking, is afraid her eye is on him. He straightens alertly and speaks in a voice that, in spite of his effort, is dripping with drowsiness.*)

TOMMY   Let me see what you wrote, Mid.

MILDRED   (*cruelly mocking*) You? You're so sleepy you couldn't see it.

TOMMY   (*valiantly*) I am not sleepy!

MRS. MILLER (*has fixed her eye on him*) My gracious, I was forgetting you were still up! You run up to bed this minute! It's hours past your bedtime!

TOMMY But it's the Fourth of July. Ain't it, Pa?

MRS. MILLER (*gives her husband an accusing stare*) There! You see what you've done? You might know he'd copy your excuses! (*Then sharply to* TOMMY) You heard what I said, Young Man!

TOMMY Aw, Ma, can't I stay up a *little* longer?

MRS. MILLER I said, no! You obey me and no more arguing about it!

TOMMY (*drags himself to his feet*) Aw! I should think I could stay up till Dick—

MILLER (*kindly but firmly*) You heard your ma say no more arguing. When she says git, you better git. (TOMMY *accepts his fate resignedly and starts around kissing them all good night.*)

TOMMY (*kissing her*) Good night, Aunt Lily.

LILY Good night, dear. Sleep well.

TOMMY (*pecking at* MILDRED) Good night, you.

MILDRED Good night, you.

TOMMY (*kissing him*) Good night, Pa.

MILLER Good night, Son. Sleep tight.

TOMMY (*kissing her*) Good night, Ma.

MRS. MILLER Good night. Here! You look feverish. Let me feel of your head. No, you're all right. Hurry up, now. And don't forget your prayers.

(TOMMY *goes slowly to the doorway—then turns suddenly, the discovery of another excuse lighting up his face.*)

TOMMY   Here's another thing, Ma. When I was up to the water closet last—

MRS. MILLER   (*sharply*) When you were *where*?

TOMMY   The bathroom.

MRS. MILLER   That's better.

TOMMY   Uncle Sid was snoring like a fog horn—and he's right next to my room. How can I ever get to sleep while he's— (*He is overcome by a jaw-cracking yawn.*)

MRS. MILLER   I guess you'd get to sleep all right if you were inside a fog horn. You run along now. (TOMMY *gives up, grins sleepily, and moves off to bed. As soon as he is off her mind, all her former uneasiness comes back on* MRS. MILLER *tenfold. She sighs, moves restlessly, then finally asks*) What time is it now, Nat?

MILLER   Now, Essie, I just told you a minute ago.

MRS. MILLER   (*resentfully*) I don't see how you can take it so calm! Here it's midnight, you might say, and our Richard still out, and we don't even know where he is.

MILDRED   I hear someone on the piazza. Bet that's him now, Ma.

MRS. MILLER   (*her anxiety immediately turning to relieved anger*) You give him a good piece of your mind, Nat, you hear me! You're too easy with him, that's the whole trouble! The idea of him daring to stay out like this! (*The front door is heard being opened and shut, and someone whistling "Waltz Me Around Again, Willie."*)

MILDRED   No, that isn't Dick. It's Art.

MRS. MILLER   (*her face falling*) Oh. (*A moment later* ARTHUR *enters through the front parlor, whistling softly, half under his breath, looking complacently pleased with himself.*)

MILLER (*surveys him over his glasses, not with enthusiasm—shortly*) So you're back, eh? We thought it was Richard.

ARTHUR Is he still out? Where'd he go to?

MILLER That's just what we'd like to know. You didn't run into him anywhere, did you?

ARTHUR No. I've been at the Rands' ever since dinner. (*He sits down in the armchair at left of table, rear.*) I suppose he sneaked off to the beach to watch the fireworks.

MILLER (*pretending an assurance he is far from feeling*) Of course. That's what we've been trying to tell your mother, but she insists on worrying her head off.

MRS. MILLER But if he was going to the fireworks, why wouldn't he say so? He knew we'd let him.

ARTHUR (*with calm wisdom*) That's easy, Ma. (*He grins superiorly.*) Didn't you hear him this morning showing off bawling out the Fourth like an anarchist? He wouldn't want to reneg on that to you—but he'd want to see the old fireworks just the same. (*He adds complacently*) I know. He's at the foolish age.

MILLER (*stares at* ARTHUR *with ill-concealed astonishment, then grins*) Well, Arthur, by gosh, you make me feel as if I owed you an apology when you talk horse sense like that. (*He turns to his wife, greatly relieved*) Arthur's hit the nail right on the head, I think, Essie. That was what I couldn't figure out—why he— but now it's clear as day.

MRS. MILLER (*with a sigh*) Well, I hope you're right. But I wish he was home.

ARTHUR (*takes out his pipe and fills and lights it with solemn gravity*) He oughtn't to be allowed out this late at his age. I wasn't, Fourth or no Fourth—if I remember.

MILLER (*a twinkle in his eyes*) Don't tax your memory trying to recall those ancient days of your youth. (MILDRED *laughs and* ARTHUR *looks sheepish. But he soon regains his aplomb.*)

ARTHUR (*importantly*) We had a corking dinner at the Rands'. We had sweetbreads on toast.

MRS. MILLER (*arising momentarily from her depression*) Just like the Rands to put on airs before you! I never could see anything to sweet-breads. Always taste like soap to me. And no real nourishment to them. I wouldn't have the pesky things on my table! (ARTHUR *again feels sat upon.*)

MILDRED (*teasingly*) Did you kiss Elsie good night?

ARTHUR Stop trying to be so darn funny all the time! You give me a pain in the ear!

MILDRED And that's where she gives me a pain, the stuck-up thing!— thinks she's the whole cheese!

MILLER (*irritably*) And that's where your everlasting wrangling gives me a pain, you two! Give us a rest! (*There is silence for a moment.*)

MRS. MILLER (*sighs worriedly again*) I do wish that boy would get home!

MILLER (*glances at her uneasily, peeks surreptitiously at his watch—then has an inspiration and turns to* ARTHUR) Arthur, what's this I hear about your having such a good singing voice? Rand was telling me he liked nothing better than to hear you sing—said you did every night you were up there. Why don't you ever give us folks at home here a treat?

ARTHUR (*pleased, but still nursing wounded dignity*) I thought you'd only sit on me.

MRS. MILLER (*perking up—proudly*) Arthur has a real nice voice. He practises when you're not at home. I didn't know you cared for singing, Nat.

MILLER Well, I do—nothing better—and when I was a boy I had a fine voice myself and folks used to say I'd ought— (*Then abruptly, mindful of his painful experience with reminiscence at dinner, looking about him guiltily*) Hmm. But don't hide your light under a bushel, Arthur. Why not give us a song or two now? You can play for him, can't you, Mildred?

MILDRED (*with a toss of her head*) I can play as well as Elsie Rand, at least!

ARTHUR (*ignoring her—clearing his throat importantly*) I've been singing a lot tonight. I don't know if my voice—

MILDRED (*forgetting her grudge, grabs her brother's hand and tugs at it*) Come on. Don't play modest. You know you're just dying to show off. (*This puts* ARTHUR *off it at once. He snatches his hand away from her angrily.*)

ARTHUR Let go of me, you! (*Then with surly dignity*) I don't feel like singing tonight, Pa. I will some other time.

MILLER You let him alone, Mildred! (*He winks at* ARTHUR, *indicating with his eyes and a nod of his head* MRS. MILLER, *who has again sunk into worried brooding. He makes it plain by this pantomime that he wants him to sing to distract his mother's mind.*)

ARTHUR (*puts aside his pipe and gets up promptly*) Oh—sure, I'll do the best I can. (*He follows* MILDRED *into the front parlor, where he switches on the lights.*)

MILLER (*to his wife*) It won't keep Tommy awake. Nothing could. And Sid, he'd sleep through an earthquake. (*Then suddenly, looking through the front parlor—grumpily*) Darn it, speak of the devil,

here he comes. Well, he's had a good sleep and he'd ought to be sobered up. (LILY *gets up from her chair and looks around her huntedly, as if for a place to hide.* MILLER *says soothingly*) Lily, you just sit down and read your book and don't pay any attention to him. (*She sits down again and bends over her book tensely. From the front parlor comes the tinkling of a piano as* MILDRED *runs over the scales. In the midst of this,* SID *enters through the front parlor. All the effervescence of his jag has worn off and he is now suffering from a bad case of hangover—nervous, sick, a prey to gloomy remorse and bitter feelings of self-loathing and self-pity. His eyes are bloodshot and puffed, his face bloated, the fringe of hair around his baldness tousled and tufty. He sidles into the room guiltily, his eyes shifting about, avoiding looking at anyone.*)

SID (*forcing a sickly, twitching smile*) Hello.

MILLER (*considerately casual*) Hello, Sid. Had a good nap? (*Then, as* SID *swallows hard and is about to break into further speech,* MILDRED'S *voice comes from the front parlor,* "I haven't played that in ever so long, but I'll try," *and she starts an accompaniment.* MILLER *motions* SID *to be quiet.*) Ssshh! Arthur's going to sing for us. (SID *flattens himself against the edge of the bookcase at center, rear, miserably self-conscious and ill-at-ease there but nervously afraid to move anywhere else.* ARTHUR *begins to sing. He has a fairly decent voice but his method is untrained sentimentality to a dripping degree. He sings that old sentimental favorite,* "Then You'll Remember Me." *The effect on his audience is instant.* MILLER *gazes before him with a ruminating melancholy, his face seeming to become gently sorrowful and old.* MRS. MILLER *stares before her, her expression becoming more and more doleful.* LILY *forgets to pretend to read her book but looks over it, her face growing tragically sad. As for* SID, *he is moved to his remorseful, guilt-*

stricken depths. His mouth pulls down at the corners and he seems about to cry. The song comes to an end. MILLER *starts, then claps his hands enthusiastically and calls)* Well done, Arthur—well done! Why, you've got a splendid voice! Give us some more! You liked that, didn't you, Essie?

MRS. MILLER *(dolefully)* Yes—but it's sad—terrible sad.

SID *(after swallowing hard, suddenly blurts out)* Nat and Essie—and Lily—I—I want to apologize—for coming home—the way I did —there's no excuse—but I didn't mean—

MILLER *(sympathetically)* Of course, Sid. It's all forgotten.

MRS. MILLER *(rousing herself—affectionately pitying)* Don't be a goose, Sid. We know how it is with picnics. You forget it. *(His face lights up a bit but his gaze shifts to* LILY *with a mute appeal, hoping for a word from her which is not forthcoming. Her eyes are fixed on her book, her body tense and rigid.)*

SID *(finally blurts out desperately)* Lily—I'm sorry—about the fireworks. Can you—forgive me? *(But* LILY *remains implacably silent. A stricken look comes over* SID's *face. In the front parlor* MILDRED *is heard saying* "But I only know the chorus"—*and she starts another accompaniment.)*

MILLER *(comes to* SID's *rescue)* Ssshh! We're going to have another song. Sit down, Sid. *(*SID, *hanging his head, flees to the farthest corner, left, front, and sits at the end of the sofa, facing front, hunched up, elbows on knees, face in hands, his round eyes childishly wounded and woe-begone.* ARTHUR *sings the popular* "Dearie," *playing up its sentimental values for all he is worth. The effect on his audience is that of the previous song, intensified—especially upon* SID. *As he finishes,* MILLER *again starts and applauds.)* Mighty fine, Arthur! You sang that darned well! Didn't he, Essie?

MRS. MILLER (*dolefully*) Yes—But I wish he wouldn't sing such sad songs. (*Then, her lips trembling*) Richard's always whistling that.

MILLER (*hastily—calls*) Give us something cheery, next one, Arthur. You know, just for variety's sake.

SID (*suddenly turns toward* LILY—*his voice choked with tears—in a passion of self-denunciation*) You're right, Lily!—right not to forgive me!—I'm no good and never will be!—I'm a no-good drunken bum!—you shouldn't even wipe your feet on me!—I'm a dirty, rotten drunk!—no good to myself or anybody else!—if I had any guts I'd kill myself, and good riddance!—but I haven't!—I'm yellow, too!—a yellow, drunken bum! (*He hides his face in his hands and begins to sob like a sick little boy. This is too much for* LILY. *All her bitter hurt and steely resolve to ignore and punish him vanish in a flash, swamped by a pitying love for him. She runs and puts her arm around him—even kisses him tenderly and impulsively on his bald head, and soothes him as if he were a little boy.* MRS. MILLER, *almost equally moved, has half risen to go to her brother, too, but* MILLER *winks and shakes his head vigorously and motions her to sit down.*)

LILY There! Don't cry, Sid! I can't bear it! Of course, I forgive you! Haven't I always forgiven you? I know you're not to blame— So don't, Sid!

SID (*lifts a tearful, humbly grateful, pathetic face to her—but a face that the dawn of a cleansed conscience is already beginning to restore to its natural puckish expression*) Do you really forgive me— I know I don't deserve it—can you really—?

LILY (*gently*) I told you I did, Sid—and I do.

SID (*kisses her hand humbly, like a big puppy licking it*) Thanks, Lily. I can't tell you— (*In the front parlor,* ARTHUR *begins to sing rollickingly "Waiting at the Church," and after the first line or two* MILDRED *joins in.* SID's *face lights up with appreciation and, automatically, he begins to tap one foot in time, still holding fast to* LILY's *hand. When they come to "sent around a note, this is what he wrote," he can no longer resist, but joins in a shaky bawl)* "Can't get away to marry you today, My wife won't let me!" (*As the song finishes, the two in the other room laugh.* MILLER *and* SID *laugh.* LILY *smiles at* SID's *laughter. Only* MRS. MILLER *remains dolefully preoccupied, as if she hadn't heard.)*

MILLER   That's fine, Arthur and Mildred. That's darned good.

SID   (*turning to* LILY *enthusiastically*) You ought to hear Vesta Victoria sing that! Gosh, she's great! I heard her at Hammerstein's Victoria—you remember, that trip I made to New York.

LILY   (*her face suddenly tired and sad again—for her memory of certain aspects of that trip is the opposite from what he would like her to recall at this moment—gently disengaging her hand from his—with a hopeless sigh*) Yes, I remember, Sid. (*He is overcome momentarily by guilty confusion. She goes quietly and sits down in her chair again. In the front parlor, from now on,* MILDRED *keeps starting to run over popular tunes but always gets stuck and turns to another.*)

MRS. MILLER   (*suddenly*) What time is it now, Nat? (*Then without giving him a chance to answer*) Oh, I'm getting worried something dreadful, Nat! You don't know what might have happened to Richard! You read in the papers every day about boys getting run over by automobiles.

LILY   Oh, don't say that, Essie!

MILLER   (*sharply, to conceal his own reawakened apprehension*) Don't get to imagining things, now!

MRS. MILLER Well, why couldn't it happen, with everyone that owns one out tonight, and lots of those driving, drunk? Or he might have gone down to the beach dock, and fallen overboard! (*On the verge of hysteria*) Oh, I know something dreadful's happened! And you can sit there listening to songs and laughing as if— Why don't you do something? Why don't you go out and find him? (*She bursts into tears.*)

LILY (*comes to her quickly and puts her arm around her*) Essie, you mustn't worry so! You'll make yourself sick! Richard's all right. I've got a feeling in my bones he's all right.

MILDRED (*comes hurrying in from the front parlor*) What's the trouble? (ARTHUR *appears in the doorway beside her. She goes to her mother and also puts an arm around her.*) Ah, don't cry, Ma! Dick'll turn up in a minute or two, wait and see!

ARTHUR Sure, he will!

MILLER (*has gotten to his feet, frowning—soberly*) I was going out to look —if he wasn't back by twelve sharp. That'd be the time it'd take him to walk from the beach if he left after the last car. But I'll go now, if it'll ease your mind. I'll take the auto and drive out the beach road—and likely pick him up on the way. (*He has taken his collar and tie from where they hang from one corner of the bookcase at rear, center, and is starting to put them on.*) You better come with me, Arthur.

ARTHUR Sure thing, Pa. (*Suddenly he listens and says*) Ssshh! There's someone on the piazza now—coming around to this door, too. That must be him. No one else would—

MRS. MILLER Oh, thank God, thank God!

MILLER (*with a sheepish smile*) Darn him! I've a notion to give him hell for worrying us all like this. (*The screen door is pushed violently open and* RICHARD *lurches in and stands swaying a little, blinking his eyes in the light. His face is a pasty pallor, shining with perspiration, and his eyes are glassy. The knees of his trousers are dirty, one of them torn from the sprawl on the sidewalk he had taken, following the* BARTENDER's *kick. They all gape at him, too paralyzed for a moment to say anything.*)

MRS. MILLER Oh, God, what's happened to him! He's gone crazy! Richard!

SID (*the first to regain presence of mind—with a grin*) Crazy, nothing. He's only soused!

ARTHUR He's drunk, that's what! (*Then shocked and condemning*) You've got your nerve! You fresh kid! We'll take that out of you when we get you down to Yale!

RICHARD (*with a wild gesture of defiance—maudlinly dramatic*)

> "Yesterday this Day's Madness did prepare
> Tomorrow's Silence, Triumph, or Despair.
> Drink! for—"

MILLER (*his face grown stern and angry, takes a threatening step toward him*) Richard! How dare—!

MRS. MILLER (*hysterically*) Don't you strike him, Nat! Don't you—!

SID (*grabbing his arm*) Steady, Nat! Keep your temper! No good bawling him out now! He don't know what he's doing!

MILLER (*controlling himself and looking a bit ashamed*) All right—you're right, Sid.

RICHARD (*drunkenly glorying in the sensation he is creating—recites with dramatic emphasis*) "And then—I will come—with vine leaves in my hair!" (*He laughs with a double-dyed sardonicism.*)

MRS. MILLER (*staring at him as if she couldn't believe her eyes*) Richard! You're intoxicated!—you bad, wicked boy, you!

RICHARD (*forces a wicked leer to his lips and quotes with ponderous mockery*) "Fancy that, Hedda!" (*Then suddenly his whole expression changes, his pallor takes on a greenish, sea-sick tinge, his eyes seem to be turned inward uneasily—and, all pose gone, he calls to his mother appealingly, like a sick little boy*) Ma! I feel—rotten! (MRS. MILLER *gives a cry and starts to go to him, but* SID *steps in her way.*)

SID You let me take care of him, Essie. I know this game backwards.

MILLER (*putting his arm around his wife*) Yes, you leave him to Sid.

SID (*his arm around* RICHARD—*leading him off through the front parlor*) Come on, Old Sport! Upstairs we go! Your old Uncle Sid'll fix you up. He's the kid that wrote the book!

MRS. MILLER (*starting after them—still aghast*) Oh, it's too terrible! Imagine our Richard! And did you hear him talking about some Hedda? Oh, I know he's been with one of those bad women, I know he has—my Richard! (*She hides her face on* MILLER's *shoulder and sobs heartbrokenly.*)

MILLER (*a tired, harassed, deeply worried look on his face—soothing her*) Now, now, you mustn't get to imagining such things! You mustn't, Essie! (LILY *and* MILDRED *and* ARTHUR *are standing about awkwardly with awed, shocked faces.*)

Curtain

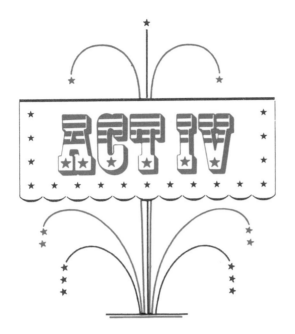

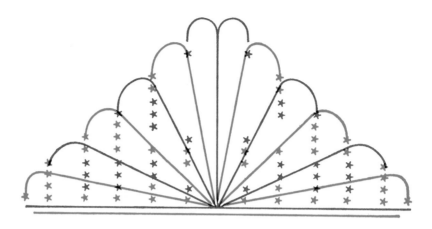

Scene I

THE SAME—*sitting-room of the Miller house—about one o'clock in the afternoon of the following day.*

As the curtain rises, the family, with the exception of RICHARD, *are discovered coming in through the back parlor from dinner in the dining-room.* MILLER *and his wife come first. His face is set in an expression of frowning severity.* MRS. MILLER'S *face is drawn and worried. She has evidently had no rest yet from a sleepless, tearful night.* SID *is himself again, his expression as innocent as if nothing had occurred the previous day that remotely concerned him. And, outside of eyes that are bloodshot and nerves that are shaky, he shows no after-effects except that he is terribly sleepy.* LILY *is gently sad and depressed.* ARTHUR *is self-consciously a virtuous young man against whom nothing can be said.* MILDRED *and* TOMMY *are subdued, covertly watching their father.*

They file into the sitting-room in silence and then stand around uncertainly, as if each were afraid to be the first to sit down. The atmosphere is as stiltedly grave as if they were attending a funeral service. Their eyes keep fixed on the head of the house, who has gone to the window at right and is staring out frowningly, savagely chewing a toothpick.

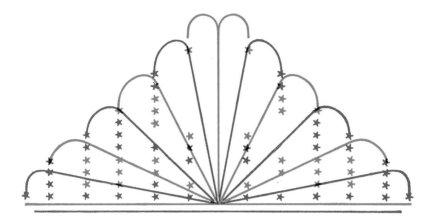

MILLER (*finally—irritably*) Damn it, I'd ought to be back at the office putting in some good licks! I've a whole pile of things that have got to be done today!

MRS. MILLER (*accusingly*) You don't mean to tell me you're going back without seeing him? It's your *duty*—!

MILLER (*exasperatedly*) 'Course I'm not! I wish you'd stop jumping to conclusions! What else did I come home for, I'd like to know? Do I usually come way back here for dinner on a busy day? I was only wishing this hadn't come up—just at this particular time. (*He ends up very lamely and is irritably conscious of the fact.*)

TOMMY (*who has been fidgeting restlessly—unable to bear the suspense a moment longer*) What is it Dick done? Why is everyone scared to tell me?

MILLER (*seizes this as an escape valve—turns and fixes his youngest son with a stern forbidding eye*) Young man, I've never spanked you yet, but that don't mean I never will! Seems to me that you've been just itching for it lately! You keep your mouth shut till you're spoken to—or I warn you something's going to happen!

MRS. MILLER Yes, Tommy, you keep still and don't bother your pa. (*Then warningly to her husband*) Careful what you say, Nat. Little pitchers have big ears.

MILLER (*peremptorily*) You kids skedaddle—all of you. Why are you always hanging around the house? Go out and play in the yard, or take a walk, and get some fresh air. (MILDRED *takes* TOMMY's *hand and leads him out through the front parlor.* ARTHUR *hangs back, as if the designation "kids" couldn't possibly apply to him. His father notices this—impatiently*) You, too, Arthur. (ARTHUR *goes out with a stiff, wounded dignity.*)

LILY (*tactfully*) I think I'll go for a walk, too. (*She goes out through the front parlor.* SID *makes a movement as if to follow her.*)

MILLER I'd like you to stay, Sid—for a while, anyway.

SID Sure (*He sits down in the rocking-chair at right, rear, of table and immediately yawns.*) Gosh, I'm dead. Don't know what's the matter with me today. Can't seem to keep awake.

MILLER (*with caustic sarcasm*) Maybe that demon chowder you drank at the picnic poisoned you! (SID *looks sheepish and forces a grin. Then* MILLER *turns to his wife with the air of one who determinedly faces the unpleasant.*) Where is Richard?

MRS. MILLER (*flusteredly*) He's still in bed. I made him stay in bed to punish him—and I thought he ought to, anyway, after being so sick. But he says he feels all right.

SID (*with another yawn*) 'Course he does. When you're young you can stand anything without it fazing you. Why, I remember when I could come down on the morning after, fresh as a daisy, and eat a breakfast of pork chops and fried onions and— (*He stops guiltily.*)

MILLER *(bitingly)* I suppose that was before eating lobster shells had ruined your iron constitution!

MRS. MILLER *(regards her brother severely)* If I was in your shoes, I'd keep still! *(Then turning to her husband)* Richard must be feeling better. He ate all the dinner I sent up, Norah says.

MILLER I thought you weren't going to give him any dinner—to punish him.

MRS. MILLER *(guiltily)* Well—in his weakened condition—I thought it best— *(Then defensively)* But you needn't think I haven't punished him. I've given him pieces of my mind he won't forget in a hurry. And I've kept reminding him his real punishment was still to come—that you were coming home to dinner on purpose —and then he'd learn that you could be terrible stern when he did such awful things.

MILLER *(stirs uncomfortably)* Hmm!

MRS. MILLER And that's just what it's your duty to do—punish him good and hard! The idea of him daring—*(Then hastily)* But you be careful how you go about it, Nat. Remember he's like you inside—too sensitive for his own good. And he never would have done it, I know, if it hadn't been for that darned little dunce, Muriel, and her numbskull father—and then all of us teasing him and hurting his feelings all day—and then you lost your temper and were so sharp with him right after dinner before he went out.

MILLER *(resentfully)* I see this is going to work round to where it's all my fault!

MRS. MILLER Now, I didn't say that, did I? Don't go losing your temper again. And here's another thing. You know as well as I, Richard would never have done such a thing alone. Why, he wouldn't know how! He must have been influenced and led by someone.

MILLER　Yes, I believe that. Did you worm out of him who it was? (*Then angrily*) By God, I'll make whoever it was regret it!

MRS. MILLER　No, he wouldn't admit there was anyone. (*Then triumphantly*) But there is one thing I did worm out of him—and I can tell you it relieved my mind more'n anything. You know, I was afraid he'd been with one of those bad women. Well, turns out there wasn't any Hedda. She was just out of those books he's been reading. He swears he's never known a Hedda in his life. And I believe him. Why, he seemed disgusted with me for having such a notion. (*Then lamely*) So somehow—I can't kind of feel it's all as bad as I thought it was. (*Then quickly and indignantly*) But it's enough, goodness knows—and you punish him good just the same. The idea of a boy his age—! Shall I go up now and tell him to get dressed, you want to see him?

MILLER　(*helplessly—and irritably*) Yes! I can't waste all day listening to you!

MRS. MILLER　(*worriedly*) Now you keep your temper, Nat, remember! (*She goes out through the front parlor.*)

MILLER　Darn women, anyway! They always get you mixed up. Their minds simply don't know what logic is! (*Then he notices that* SID *is dozing—sharply*) Sid!

SID　(*blinking—mechanically*) I'll take the same. (*Then hurriedly*) What'd you say, Nat?

MILLER　(*caustically*) What I didn't say was what'll you have. (*Irritably*) Do you want to be of some help, or don't you? Then keep awake and try and use your brains! This is a damned sight more serious than Essie has any idea! She thinks there weren't any girls mixed up with Richard's spree last night—but I happen to know there were! (*He takes a letter from his pocket.*) Here's a

note a woman left with one of the boys downstairs at the office this morning—didn't ask to see me, just said give me this. He'd never seen her before—said she looked like a tart. (*He has opened the letter and reads*) "Your son got the booze he drank last night at the Pleasant Beach House. The bartender there knew he was under age but served him just the same. He thought it was a good joke to get him soused. If you have any guts you will run that bastard out of town." Well, what do you think of that? It's a woman's handwriting—not signed, of course.

SID She's one of the babies, all right—judging from her elegant language.

MILLER See if you recognize the handwriting.

SID (*with a reproachful look*) Nat, I resent the implication that I correspond with all the tramps around this town. (*Looking at the letter*) No, I don't know who this one could be. (*Handing the letter back*) But I deduce that the lady had a run-in with the barkeep and wants revenge.

MILLER (*grimly*) And I deduce that before that she must have picked up Richard—or how would she know who he was?—and took him to this dive.

SID Maybe. The Pleasant Beach House is nothing but a bed house— (*Quickly*) At least, so I've been told.

MILLER That's just the sort of damned fool thing he might do to spite Muriel, in the state of mind he was in—pick up some tart. And she'd try to get him drunk so—

SID Yes, it might have happened like that—and it might not. How're we ever going to prove it? Everyone at the Pleasant Beach will lie their heads off.

MILLER (*simply and proudly*) Richard won't lie.

SID Well, don't blame him if he don't remember everything that happened last night. (*Then sincerely concerned*) I hope you're wrong, Nat. That kind of baby is dangerous for a kid like Dick— in more ways than one. You know what I mean.

MILLER (*frowningly*) Yep—and that's just what's got me worried. Damn it, I've got to have a straight talk with him—about women and all those things. I ought to have long ago.

SID Yes. You ought.

MILLER I've tried to a couple of times. I did it all right with Wilbur and Lawrence and Arthur, when it came time—but, hell, with Richard I always get sort of ashamed of myself and can't get started right. You feel, in spite of all his bold talk out of books, that he's so darned innocent inside.

SID I know. I wouldn't like the job. (*Then after a pause—curiously*) How were you figuring to punish him for his sins?

MILLER (*frowning*) To be honest with you, Sid, I'm damned if I know. All depends on what I feel about what he feels when I first size him up—and then it'll be like shooting in the dark.

SID If I didn't know you so well, I'd say don't be too hard on him. (*He smiles a little bitterly.*) If you remember, I was always getting punished—and see what a lot of good it did me!

MILLER (*kindly*) Oh, there's lots worse than you around, so don't take to boasting. (*Then, at a sound from the front parlor—with a sigh*) Well, here comes the Bad Man, I guess.

SID (*getting up*) I'll beat it. (*But it is* MRS. MILLER *who appears in the doorway, looking guilty and defensive.* SID *sits down again.*)

MRS. MILLER   I'm sorry, Nat—but he was sound asleep and I didn't have the heart to wake him. I waited for him to wake up but he didn't.

MILLER   (concealing a relief of which he is ashamed—exasperatedly) Well, I'll be double damned! If you're not the—

MRS. MILLER   (defensively aggressive) Now don't lose your temper at me, Nat Miller! You know as well as I do he needs all the sleep he can get today—after last night's ructions! Do you want him to be taken down sick? And what difference does it make to you anyway? You can see him when you come home for supper, can't you? My goodness, I never saw you so savage-tempered! You'd think you couldn't bear waiting to punish him!

MILLER   (outraged) Well, I'll be eternally—(Then suddenly he laughs.) No use talking, you certainly take the cake! But you know darned well I told you I'm not coming home to supper tonight. I've got a date with Jack Lawson that may mean a lot of new advertising and it's important.

MRS. MILLER   Then you can see him when you do come home.

MILLER   (covering his evident relief at this respite with a fuming manner) All right! All right! I give up! I'm going back to the office. (He starts for the front parlor) Bring a man all the way back here on a busy day and then you— No consideration— (He disappears, and a moment later the front door is heard shutting behind him.)

MRS. MILLER   Well! I never saw Nat so bad-tempered.

SID   (with a chuckle) Bad temper, nothing. He's so tickled to get out of it for a while he can't see straight!

MRS. MILLER   (with a sniff) I hope I know him better than you. (Then fussing about the room, setting this and that in place, while SID yawns drowsily and blinks his eyes) Sleeping like a baby—so innocent-looking. You'd think butter wouldn't melt in his mouth. It all goes to show you never can tell by appearances—not even when it's your own child. The idea!

SID *(drowsily)* Oh, Dick's all right, Essie. Stop worrying.

MRS. MILLER *(with a sniff)* Of course, you'd say that. I suppose you'll have him out with you painting the town red the next thing! *(As she is talking,* RICHARD *appears in the doorway from the sitting-room. He shows no ill effects from his experience the night before. In fact, he looks surprisingly healthy. He is dressed in old clothes that look as if they had been hurriedly flung on. His expression is one of hang-dog guilt mingled with a defensive defiance.)*

RICHARD *(with self-conscious unconcern, ignoring his mother)* Hello, Sid.

MRS. MILLER *(whirls on him)* What are you doing here, Young Man? I thought you were asleep! Seems to me you woke up pretty quick—just after your pa left the house!

RICHARD *(sulkily)* I wasn't asleep. I heard you in the room.

MRS. MILLER *(outraged)* Do you mean to say you were deliberately deceiving—

RICHARD I wasn't deceiving. You didn't ask if I was asleep.

MRS. MILLER It amounts to the same thing and you know it! It isn't enough your wickedness last night, but now you have to take to lying!

RICHARD I wasn't lying, Ma. If you'd asked if I was asleep I'd have said no.

MRS. MILLER I've a good mind to send you straight back to bed and make you stay there!

RICHARD Ah, what for, Ma? It was only giving me a headache, lying there.

MRS. MILLER   If you've got a headache, I guess you know it doesn't come from that! And imagine me standing there, and feeling sorry for you, like a fool—even having a run-in with your pa because—But you wait till he comes back tonight! If you don't catch it!

RICHARD   (*sulkily*) I don't care.

MRS. MILLER   You don't care? You talk as if you weren't sorry for what you did last night!

RICHARD   (*defiantly*) I'm not sorry.

MRS. MILLER   Richard! You ought to be ashamed! I'm beginning to think you're hardened in wickedness, that's what!

RICHARD   (*with bitter despondency*) I'm not sorry because I don't care a darn what I did, or what's done to me, or anything about anything! I won't do it again—

MRS. MILLER   (*seizing on this to relent a bit*) Well, I'm glad to hear you say that, anyway!

RICHARD   But that's not because I think it was wicked or any such old-fogy moral notion, but because it wasn't any fun. It didn't make me happy and funny like it does Uncle Sid—

SID   (*drowsily*) What's that? Who's funny?

RICHARD   (*ignoring him*) It only made me sadder—and sick—so I don't see any sense in it.

MRS. MILLER   Now you're talking sense! That's a good boy.

RICHARD   But I'm not sorry I tried it once—curing the soul by means of the senses, as Oscar Wilde says. (*Then with despairing pessimism*) But what does it matter what I do or don't do? Life is all a stupid farce! I'm through with it! (*With a sinister smile*) It's lucky there aren't any of General Gabler's pistols around—or you'd see if I'd stand it much longer!

MRS. MILLER (*worriedly impressed by this threat—but pretending scorn*) I don't know anything about General Gabler—I suppose that's more of those darned books—but you're a silly gabbler yourself when you talk that way!

RICHARD (*darkly*) That's how little you know about me.

MRS. MILLER (*giving in to her worry*) I wish you wouldn't say those terrible things—about life and pistols! You don't want to worry me to death, do you?

RICHARD (*reassuringly stoical now*) You needn't worry, Ma. It was only my despair talking. But I'm not a coward. I'll face—my fate.

MRS. MILLER (*stands looking at him puzzledly—then gives it up with a sigh*) Well, all I can say is you're the queerest boy I ever did hear of! (*Then solicitously, putting her hand on his forehead*) How's your headache? Do you want me to get you some Bromo Seltzer?

RICHARD (*taken down—disgustedly*) No, I don't! Aw, Ma, you don't understand anything!

MRS. MILLER Well, I understand this much: It's your liver, that's what! You'll take a good dose of salts tomorrow morning, and no nonsense about it! (*Then suddenly*) My goodness, I wonder what time it's getting to be. I've got to go upstreet. (*She goes to the front-parlor doorway—then turns*) You stay here, Richard, you hear? Remember, you're not allowed out today—for a punishment. (*She hurries away.* RICHARD *sits in tragic gloom.* SID, *without opening his eyes, speaks to him drowsily.*)

SID Well, how's my fellow Rum Pot, as good old Dowie calls us? Got a head?

RICHARD (*startled—sheepishly*) Aw, don't go dragging that up, Uncle Sid. I'm never going to be such a fool again, I tell you.

SID (*with drowsy cynicism—not unmixed with bitterness at the end*) Seems to me I've heard someone say that before. Who could it have been, I wonder? Why, if it wasn't Sid Davis! Yes, sir, I've heard him say that very thing a thousand times, must be. But then he's always fooling; you can't take a word he says seriously; he's a card, that Sid is!

RICHARD (*darkly*) I was desperate, Uncle—even if she wasn't worth it. I was wounded to the heart.

SID I like to the quick better myself—more stylish. (*Then sadly*) But you're right. Love is hell on a poor sucker. Don't I know it? (RICHARD *is disgusted and disdains to reply.* SID's *chin sinks on his chest and he begins to breathe noisily, fast asleep.* RICHARD *glances at him with aversion. There is a sound of someone on the porch and the screen door is opened and* MILDRED *enters. She smiles on seeing her uncle, then gives a start on seeing* RICHARD.)

MILDRED Hello! Are you allowed up?

RICHARD Of course, I'm allowed up.

MILDRED (*comes and sits in her father's chair at right, front, of table*) How did Pa punish you?

RICHARD He didn't. He went back to the office without seeing me.

MILDRED Well, you'll catch it later. (*Then rebukingly*) And you ought to. If you'd ever seen how awful you looked last night!

RICHARD Ah, forget it, can't you?

MILDRED Well, are you ever going to do it again, that's what I want to know.

RICHARD What's that to you?

MILDRED (*with suppressed excitement*) Well, if you don't solemnly swear you won't—then I won't give you something I've got for you.

RICHARD Don't try to kid me. You haven't got anything.

MILDRED I have, too.

RICHARD What?

MILDRED Wouldn't you like to know! I'll give you three guesses.

RICHARD (*with disdainful dignity*) Don't bother me. I'm in no mood to play riddles with kids!

MILDRED Oh, well, if you're going to get snippy! Anyway you haven't promised yet.

RICHARD (*a prey to keen curiosity now*) I promise. What is it?

MILDRED What would you like best in the world?

RICHARD I don't know. What?

MILDRED And you pretend to be in love! If I told Muriel that!

RICHARD (*breathlessly*) Is it—from her?

MILDRED (*laughing*) Well, I guess it's a shame to keep you guessing. Yes. It is from her. I was walking past her place just now when I saw her waving from their parlor window, and I went up and she said give this to Dick, and she didn't have a chance to say anything else because her mother called her and said she wasn't allowed to have company. So I took it—and here it is. (*She gives him a letter folded many times into a tiny square.* RICHARD *opens it with a trembling eagerness and reads.* MILDRED *watches him curiously—then sighs affectedly.*) Gee, it must be nice to be in love like you are—all with one person.

RICHARD (*his eyes shining*) Gee, Mid, do you know what she says—that she didn't mean a word in that other letter. Her old man made her write it. And she loves me and only me and always will, no matter how they punish her!

MILDRED My! I'd never think she had that much spunk.

RICHARD Huh! You don't know her! Think I could fall in love with a girl that was afraid to say her soul's her own? I should say not! (*Then more gleefully still*) And she's going to try and sneak out and meet me tonight. She says she thinks she can do it. (*Then suddenly feeling this enthusiasm before* MILDRED *is entirely the wrong note for a cynical pessimist—with an affected bitter laugh*) Ha! I knew darned well she couldn't hold out—that she'd ask to see me again. (*He misquotes cynically*) "Women never know when the curtain has fallen. They always want another act."

MILDRED Is that so, Smarty?

RICHARD (*as if he were weighing the matter*) I don't know whether I'll consent to keep this date or not.

MILDRED Well, I know! You're not allowed out, you silly! So you can't!

RICHARD (*dropping all pretense—defiantly*) Can't I, though! You wait and see if I can't! I'll see her tonight if it's the last thing I ever do! I don't care how I'm punished after!

MILDRED (*admiringly*) Goodness! I never thought you had such nerve!

RICHARD You promise to keep your face shut, Mid—until after I've left—then you can tell Pa and Ma where I've gone—I mean, if they're worrying I'm off like last night.

MILDRED All right. Only you've got to do something for me when I ask.

RICHARD 'Course I will. (*Then excitedly*) And say, Mid! Right now's the best chance for me to get away—while everyone's out! Ma'll be coming back soon and she'll keep watching me like a cat— (*He starts for the back parlor.*) I'm going. I'll sneak out the back.

MILDRED (*excitedly*) But what'll you do till nighttime? It's ages to wait.

RICHARD What do I care how long I wait! (*Intensely sincere now*) I'll think of her—and dream! I'd wait a million years and never mind it—for her! (*He gives his sister a superior scornful glance.*) The trouble with you is, you don't understand what love means! (*He disappears through the back parlor.* MILDRED *looks after him admiringly.* SID *puffs and begins to snore peacefully.*)

Curtain

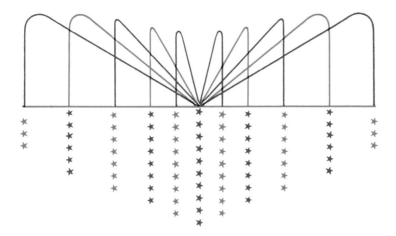

Scene II

A STRIP OF BEACH *along the harbor. At left, a bank of dark earth, running half-diagonally back along the beach, marking the line where the sand of the beach ends and fertile land begins. The top of the bank is grassy and the trailing boughs of willow trees extend out over it and over a part of the beach. At left, front, is a path leading up the bank, between the willows. On the beach, at center, front, a white, flat-bottomed rowboat is drawn up, its bow about touching the bank, the painter trailing up the bank, evidently made fast to the trunk of a willow. Half-way down the sky, at rear, left, the crescent of the new moon casts a soft, mysterious, caressing light over everything. The sand of the beach shimmers palely. The forward half (left of center) of the rowboat is in the deep shadow cast by the willow, the stern section is in moonlight. In the distance, the orchestra of a summer hotel can be heard very faintly at intervals.*

RICHARD *is discovered sitting sideways on the gunwale of the rowboat near the stern. He is facing left, watching the path. He is in a great state of anxious expectancy, squirming about uncomfortably on the narrow gunwale, kicking at the sand restlessly, twirling his straw hat, with a bright-colored band in stripes, around on his finger.*

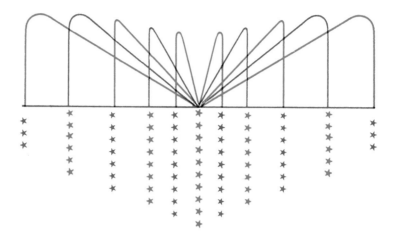

RICHARD   (*thinking aloud*) Must be nearly nine . . . I can hear the Town
Hall clock strike, it's so still tonight . . . Gee, I'll bet Ma had a fit
when she found out I'd sneaked out . . . I'll catch hell when I get
back, but it'll be worth it . . . if only Muriel turns up . . . she
didn't say for certain she could . . . gosh, I wish she'd come! . . .
am I sure she wrote nine? . . . (*He puts the straw hat on the seat
amidships and pulls the folded letter out of his pocket and peers at
it in the moonlight.*) Yes, it's nine, all right. (*He starts to put the
note back in his pocket, then stops and kisses it—then shoves it
away hastily, sheepish, looking around him shamefacedly, as if
afraid he were being observed.*) Aw, that's silly . . . no, it isn't
either . . . not when you're really in love. . . . (*He jumps to his
feet restlessly.*) Darn it, I wish she'd show up! . . . think of something else . . . that'll make the time pass quicker . . . where was I
this time last night? . . . waiting outside the Pleasant Beach
House . . . Belle . . . ah, forget her! . . . now, when Muriel's coming . . . that's a fine time to think of—! . . . but you hugged and
kissed her . . . not until I was drunk, I didn't . . . and then it was
all showing off . . . darned fool! . . . and I didn't go upstairs with
her . . . even if she was pretty . . . aw, she wasn't pretty . . . she

was all painted up . . . she was just a whore . . . she was everything dirty . . . Muriel's a million times prettier anyway . . . Muriel and I will go upstairs . . . when we're married . . . but that will be beautiful . . . but I oughtn't even to think of that yet . . . it's not right . . . I'd never—now . . . and she'd never . . . she's a decent girl . . . I couldn't love her if she wasn't . . . but after we're married. . . . (*He gives a little shiver of passionate longing—then resolutely turns his mind away from these improper, almost desecrating thoughts.*) That damned barkeep kicking me . . . I'll bet you if I hadn't been drunk I'd have given him one good punch in the nose, even if he could have licked me after! . . . (*Then with a shiver of shamefaced revulsion and self-disgust*) Aw, you deserved a kick in the pants . . . making such a darned slob of yourself . . . reciting the Ballad of Reading Gaol to those lowbrows! . . . you must have been a fine sight when you got home . . . having to be put to bed and getting sick! . . . Phaw! . . . (*He squirms disgustedly.*) Think of something else, can't you? . . . recite something . . . see if you remember . . .

> "Nay, let us walk from fire unto fire
> From passionate pain to deadlier delight—
> I am too young to live without desire,
> Too young art thou to waste this summer night—"

. . . gee, that's a peach! . . . I'll have to memorize the rest and recite it to Muriel the next time. . . . I wish I could write poetry . . . about her and me. . . . (*He sighs and stares around him at the night.*) Gee, it's beautiful tonight . . . as if it was a special night . . . for me and Muriel. . . . Gee, I love tonight. . . . I love the sand, and the trees, and the grass, and the water and the sky, and the moon . . . it's all in me and I'm in it . . . God, it's so beautiful! (*He stands staring at the moon with a rapt face. From the distance the Town Hall clock begins to strike. This brings him back to earth with a start.)* There's nine now. . . . *(He peers at the path apprehensively.)* I don't see her . . . she must have got caught. . . . *(Almost tearfully)* Gee, I hate to go home and catch hell . . . without having seen her! . . . *(Then calling a manly cynicism to his aid)* Aw, who ever heard of a woman ever being on time. . . . I ought to know enough about life by this time not to expect . . . *(Then with sudden excitement)* There she comes now. . . . Gosh! *(He heaves a huge sigh of relief—then recites dramatically to himself, his eyes on the approaching figure)*

> "And lo my love, mine own soul's heart, more dear
> Than mine own soul, more beautiful than God,
> Who hath my being between the hands of her—"

(Then hastily) Mustn't let her know I'm so tickled. . . . I ought to be mad about that first letter, anyway . . . if women are too sure of you, they treat you like slaves . . . let her suffer, for a change. . . . *(He starts to stroll around with exaggerated carelessness, turning his back on the path, hands in pockets, whistling with insouciance "Waiting at the Church."*

*(*MURIEL MC COMBER *enters from down the path, left front. She is fifteen, going on sixteen. She is a pretty girl with a plump, graceful little figure, fluffy, light-brown hair, big naïve wondering dark eyes, a round dimpled face, a melting drawly voice. Just now she is in a great thrilled state of timid adventurousness. She hesitates in the shadow at the foot of the path, waiting for* RICHARD *to see her; but he resolutely goes on whistling with back turned, and she has to call him.)*

MURIEL Oh, Dick.

RICHARD   (*turns around with an elaborate simulation of being disturbed in the midst of profound meditation*) Oh, hello. Is it nine already? Gosh, time passes—when you're thinking.

MURIEL   (*coming toward him as far as the edge of the shadow—disappointedly*) I thought you'd be waiting right here at the end of the path. I'll bet you'd forgotten I was even coming.

RICHARD   (*strolling a little toward her but not too far—carelessly*) No, I hadn't forgotten, honest. But got to thinking about life.

MURIEL   You might think of me for a change, after all the risk I've run to see you! (*Hesitating timidly on the edge of the shadow*) Dick! You come here to me. I'm afraid to go out in that bright moonlight where anyone might see me.

RICHARD   (*coming toward her—scornfully*) Aw, there you go again—always scared of life!

MURIEL   (*indignantly*) Dick Miller, I do think you've got an awful nerve to say that after all the risks I've run making this date and then sneaking out! You didn't take the trouble to sneak any letter to me, I notice!

RICHARD   No, because after your first letter, I thought everything was dead and past between us.

MURIEL   And I'll bet you didn't care one little bit! (*On the verge of humiliated tears*) Oh, I was a fool ever to come here! I've got a good notion to go right home and never speak to you again! (*She half turns back toward the path.*)

RICHARD   (*frightened—immediately becomes terribly sincere—grabbing her hand*) Aw, don't go, Muriel! Please! I didn't mean anything like that, honest, I didn't! Gee, if you knew how broken-hearted I was by that first letter, and how darned happy your second letter made me—!

MURIEL　(*happily relieved—but appreciates she has the upper hand now and doesn't relent at once*) I don't believe you.

RICHARD　You ask Mid how happy I was. She can prove it.

MURIEL　She'd say anything you told her to. I don't care anything about what she'd say. It's you. You've got to swear to me—

RICHARD　I swear!

MURIEL　(*demurely*) Well then, all right. I'll believe you.

RICHARD　(*his eyes on her face lovingly—genuine adoration in his voice*) Gosh, you're pretty tonight, Muriel! It seems ages since we've been together! If you knew how I've suffered—!

MURIEL　I did, too.

RICHARD　(*unable to resist falling into his tragic literary pose for a moment*) The despair in my soul— (*He recites dramatically*) "Something was dead in each of us, And what was dead was Hope!" That was me! My hope of happiness was dead! (*Then with sincere boyish fervor*) Gosh, Muriel, it sure is wonderful to be with you again! (*He puts a timid arm around her awkwardly.*)

MURIEL　(*shyly*) I'm glad—it makes you happy. I'm happy, too.

RICHARD　Can't I—won't you let me kiss you—now? Please! (*He bends his face toward hers.*)

MURIEL　(*ducking her head away—timidly*) No. You mustn't. Don't—

RICHARD　Aw, why can't I?

MURIEL　Because—I'm afraid.

RICHARD　(*discomfited—taking his arm from around her—a bit sulky and impatient with her*) Aw, that's what you always say! You're always so afraid! Aren't you ever going to let me?

MURIEL I will—sometime.

RICHARD When?

MURIEL Soon, maybe.

RICHARD Tonight, will you?

MURIEL (*coyly*) I'll see.

RICHARD Promise?

MURIEL I promise—maybe.

RICHARD All right. You remember you've promised. (*Then coaxingly*) Aw, don't let's stand here. Come on out and we can sit down in the boat.

MURIEL (*hesitantly*) It's so bright out there.

RICHARD No one'll see. You know there's never anyone around here at night.

MURIEL (*illogically*) I know there isn't. That's why I thought it would be the best place. But there might be someone.

RICHARD (*taking her hand and tugging at it gently*) There isn't a soul. (MURIEL *steps out a little and looks up and down fearfully.* RICHARD *goes on insistently*) Aw, what's the use of a moon if you can't see it!

MURIEL But it's only a new moon. That's not much to look at.

RICHARD But I want to see you. I can't here in the shadow. I want to—drink in—all your beauty.

MURIEL (*can't resist this*) Well, all right—only I can't stay only a few minutes. (*She lets him lead her toward the stern of the boat.*)

RICHARD (*pleadingly*) Aw, you can stay a little while, can't you? Please!

(He helps her in and she settles herself in the stern seat of the boat, facing diagonally left front.)

MURIEL A little while. *(He sits beside her.)* But I've got to be home in bed again pretending to be asleep by ten o'clock. That's the time Pa and Ma come up to bed, as regular as clock work, and Ma always looks into my room.

RICHARD But you'll have oodles of time to do that.

MURIEL *(excitedly)* Dick, you have no idea what I went through to get here tonight! My, but it was exciting! You know Pa's punishing me by sending me to bed at eight sharp, and I had to get all undressed and into bed 'cause at half-past he sends Ma up to make sure I've obeyed, and she came up, and I pretended to be asleep, and she went down again, and I got up and dressed in such a hurry—I must look a sight, don't I?

RICHARD You do not! You look wonderful!

MURIEL And then I sneaked down the back stairs. And the pesky old stairs squeaked, and my heart was in my mouth, I was so scared, and then I sneaked out through the back yard, keeping in the dark under the trees, and— My, but it was exciting! Dick, you don't realize how I've been punished for your sake. Pa's been so mean and nasty, I've almost hated him!

RICHARD And you don't realize what I've been through for you—and what I'm in for—for sneaking out—*(Then darkly)* And for what I did last night—what your letter made me do!

MURIEL *(made terribly curious by his ominous tone)* What did my letter make you do?

RICHARD *(beginning to glory in this)* It's too long a story—and let the dead past bury its dead. *(Then with real feeling)* Only it isn't past, I can tell you! What I'll catch when Pa gets hold of me!

MURIEL Tell me, Dick! Begin at the beginning and tell me!

RICHARD (*tragically*) Well, after your old—your father left our place I caught holy hell from Pa.

MURIEL Dick! You mustn't swear!

RICHARD (*somberly*) Hell is the only word that can describe it. And on top of that, to torture me more, he gave me your letter. After I'd read that I didn't want to live any more. Life seemed like a tragic farce.

MURIEL I'm so awful sorry, Dick—honest I am! But you might have known I'd never write that unless—

RICHARD I thought your love for me was dead. I thought you'd never loved me, that you'd only been cruelly mocking me—to torture me!

MURIEL Dick! I'd never! You know I'd never!

RICHARD I wanted to die. I sat and brooded about death. Finally I made up my mind I'd kill myself.

MURIEL (*excitedly*) Dick! You didn't!

RICHARD I did, too! If there'd been one of Hedda Gabler's pistols around, you'd have seen if I wouldn't have done it beautifully! I thought, when I'm dead, she'll be sorry she ruined my life!

MURIEL (*cuddling up a little to him*) If you ever had! I'd have died, too! Honest, I would!

RICHARD But suicide is the act of a coward. That's what stopped me. (*Then with a bitter change of tone*) And anyway, I thought to myself, she isn't worth it.

MURIEL (*huffily*) That's a nice thing to say!

RICHARD Well, if you meant what was in the letter, you wouldn't have been worth it, would you?

MURIEL But I've told you Pa—

RICHARD So I said to myself, I'm through with women; they're all alike!

MURIEL I'm not.

RICHARD And I thought, what difference does it make what I do now? I might as well forget her and lead the pace that kills, and drown my sorrows! You know I had eleven dollars saved up to buy you something for your birthday, but I thought, she's dead to me now and why shouldn't I throw it away? (*Then hastily*) I've still got almost five left, Muriel, and I can get you something nice with that.

MURIEL (*excitedly*) What do I care about your old presents? You tell me what you did!

RICHARD (*darkly again*) After it was dark, I sneaked out and went to a low dive I know about.

MURIEL Dick Miller, I don't believe you ever!

RICHARD You ask them at the Pleasant Beach House if I didn't! They won't forget me in a hurry!

MURIEL (*impressed and horrified*) You went there? Why, that's a terrible place! Pa says it ought to be closed by the police!

RICHARD (*darkly*) I said it was a dive, didn't I? It's a "secret house of shame." And they let me into a secret room behind the bar-room. There wasn't anyone there but a Princeton Senior I know —he belongs to Tiger Inn and he's fullback on the football team —and he had two chorus girls from New York with him, and they were all drinking champagne.

MURIEL (*disturbed by the entrance of the chorus girls*) Dick Miller! I hope you didn't notice—

RICHARD (*carelessly*) I had a highball by myself and then I noticed one of the girls—the one that wasn't with the fullback—looking at me. She had strange-looking eyes. And then she asked me if I wouldn't drink champagne with them and come and sit with her.

MURIEL She must have been a nice thing! (*Then a bit falteringly*) And did—you?

RICHARD (*with tragic bitterness*) Why shouldn't I, when you'd told me in that letter you'd never see me again?

MURIEL (*almost tearfully*) But you ought to have known Pa made me—

RICHARD I didn't know that then. (*Then rubbing it in*) Her name was Belle. She had yellow hair—the kind that burns and stings you!

MURIEL I'll bet it was dyed!

RICHARD She kept smoking one cigarette after another—but that's nothing for a chorus girl.

MURIEL (*indignantly*) She was low and bad, that's what she was or she couldn't be a chorus girl, and her smoking cigarettes proves it! (*Then falteringly again*) And then what happened?

RICHARD (*carelessly*) Oh, we just kept drinking champagne—I bought a round—and then I had a fight with the barkeep and knocked him down because he'd insulted her. He was a great big thug but—

MURIEL (*huffily*) I don't see how he could—insult that kind! And why did you fight for her? Why didn't the Princeton fullback who'd brought them there? He must have been bigger than you.

RICHARD (*stopped for a moment—then quickly*) He was too drunk by that time.

MURIEL   And were you drunk?

RICHARD   Only a little then. I was worse later. (*Proudly*) You ought to have seen me when I got home! I was on the verge of delirium tremens!

MURIEL   I'm glad I didn't see you. You must have been awful. I hate people who get drunk. I'd have hated you!

RICHARD   Well, it was all your fault, wasn't it? If you hadn't written that letter—

MURIEL   But I've told you I didn't mean— (*Then faltering but fascinated*) But what happened with that Belle—after—before you went home?

RICHARD   Oh, we kept drinking champagne and she said she'd fallen in love with me at first sight and she came and sat on my lap and kissed me.

MURIEL   (*stiffening*) Oh!

RICHARD   (*quickly, afraid he has gone too far*) But it was only all in fun, and then we just kept on drinking champagne, and finally I said good night and came home.

MURIEL   And did you kiss her?

RICHARD   No, I didn't.

MURIEL   (*distractedly*) You did, too! You're lying and you know it. You did, too! (*Then tearfully*) And there I was right at that time lying in bed not able to sleep, wondering how I was ever going to see you again and crying my eyes out, while you—! (*She suddenly jumps to her feet in a tearful fury.*) I hate you! I wish you were dead! I'm going home this minute! I never want to lay eyes on you again! And this time I mean it! (*She tries to jump out of the boat but he holds her back. All the pose has dropped from him now and he is in a frightened state of contrition.*)

RICHARD (*imploringly*) Muriel! Wait! Listen!

MURIEL I don't want to listen! Let me go! If you don't I'll bite your hand!

RICHARD I won't let you go! You've got to let me explain! I never—! Ouch! (*For* MURIEL *has bitten his hand and it hurts, and, stung by the pain, he lets go instinctively, and she jumps quickly out of the boat and starts running toward the path.* RICHARD *calls after her with bitter despair and hurt*) All right! Go if you want to—if you haven't the decency to let me explain! I hate you too! I'll go and see Belle!

MURIEL (*seeing he isn't following her, stops at the foot of the path—defiantly*) Well, go and see her—if that's the kind of girl you like! What do I care? (*Then as he only stares before him broodingly, sitting dejectedly in the stern of the boat, a pathetic figure of injured grief*) You can't explain! What can you explain? You owned up you kissed her!

RICHARD I did not. I said she kissed me.

MURIEL (*scornfully, but drifting back a step in his direction*) And I suppose you just sat and let yourself be kissed! Tell that to the Marines!

RICHARD (*injuredly*) All right! If you're going to call me a liar every word I say—

MURIEL (*drifting back another step*) I didn't call you a liar. I only meant—it sounds fishy. Don't you know it does?

RICHARD I don't know anything. I only know I wish I was dead!

MURIEL (*gently reproving*) You oughtn't to say that. It's wicked. (*Then after a pause*) And I suppose you'll tell me you didn't fall in love with her?

RICHARD   (*scornfully*) I should say not! Fall in love with that kind of girl! What do you take me for?

MURIEL   (*practically*) How do you know what you did if you drank so much champagne?

RICHARD   I kept my head—with her. I'm not a sucker, no matter what you think!

MURIEL   (*drifting nearer*) Then you didn't—love her?

RICHARD   I hated her! She wasn't even pretty! And I had a fight with her before I left, she got so fresh. I told her I loved you and never could love anyone else, and for her to leave me alone.

MURIEL   But you said just now you were going to see her—

RICHARD   That was only bluff. I wouldn't—unless you left me. Then I wouldn't care what I did—any more than I did last night. (*Then suddenly defiant*) And what if I did kiss her once or twice? I only did it to get back at you!

MURIEL   Dick!

RICHARD   You're a fine one to blame me—when it was all your fault! Why can't you be fair? Didn't I think you were out of my life forever? Hadn't you written me you were? Answer me that!

MURIEL   But I've told you a million times that Pa—

RICHARD   Why didn't you have more sense than to let him make you write it? Was it my fault you didn't?

MURIEL   It was your fault for being so stupid! You ought to have known he stood right over me and told me each word to write. If I'd refused, it would only have made everything worse. I had to pretend, so I'd get a chance to see you. Don't you see, Silly? And I had sand enough to sneak out to meet you tonight, didn't I? (*He doesn't answer. She moves nearer.*) Still I can see how you

felt the way you did—and maybe I am to blame for that. So I'll forgive and forget, Dick—if you'll swear to me you didn't even think of loving that—

RICHARD *(eagerly)* I didn't! I swear, Muriel. I couldn't. I love you!

MURIEL Well, then—I still love you.

RICHARD Then come back here, why don't you?

MURIEL *(coyly)* It's getting late.

RICHARD It's not near half-past yet.

MURIEL *(comes back and sits down by him shyly)* All right—only I'll have to go soon, Dick. *(He puts his arm around her. She cuddles up close to him.)* I'm sorry—I hurt your hand.

RICHARD That was nothing. It felt wonderful—even to have you bite!

MURIEL *(impulsively takes his hand and kisses it)* There! That'll cure it. *(She is overcome by confusion at her boldness.)*

RICHARD You shouldn't—waste that—on my hand. *(Then tremblingly)* You said—you'd let me—

MURIEL I said, maybe.

RICHARD Please, Muriel. You know—I want it so!

MURIEL Will it wash off—her kisses—make you forget you ever—for always?

RICHARD I should say so! I'd never remember—anything but it—never want anything but it—ever again.

MURIEL *(shyly lifting her lips)* Then—all right—Dick. *(He kisses her tremblingly and for a moment their lips remain together. Then she lets her head sink on his shoulder and sighs softly.)* The moon is beautiful, isn't it?

RICHARD (*kissing her hair*) Not as beautiful as you! Nothing is! (*Then after a pause*) Won't it be wonderful when we're married?

MURIEL Yes—but it's so long to wait.

RICHARD Perhaps I needn't go to Yale. Perhaps Pa will give me a job. Then I'd soon be making enough to—

MURIEL You better do what your pa thinks best—and I'd like you to be at Yale. (*Then patting his face*) Poor you! Do you think he'll punish you awful?

RICHARD (*intensely*) I don't know and I don't care! Nothing would have kept me from seeing you tonight—not if I'd had to crawl over red-hot coals! (*Then falling back on Swinburne—but with passionate sincerity*) You have my being between the hands of you! You are "my love, mine own soul's heart, more dear than mine own soul, more beautiful than God!"

MURIEL (*shocked and delighted*) Ssshh! It's wrong to say that.

RICHARD (*adoringly*) Gosh, but I love you! Gosh, I love you—Darling!

MURIEL I love you, too—Sweetheart! (*They kiss. Then she lets her head sink on his shoulder again and they both sit in a rapt trance, staring at the moon. After a pause—dreamily*) Where'll we go on our honeymoon, Dick? To Niagara Falls?

RICHARD (*scornfully*) That dump where all the silly fools go? I should say not! (*With passionate romanticism*) No, we'll go to some far-off wonderful place! (*He calls on Kipling to help him.*) Somewhere out on the Long Trail—the trail that is always new—on the road to Mandalay! We'll watch the dawn come up like thunder out of China!

MURIEL (*hazily but happily*) That'll be wonderful, won't it?

Curtain

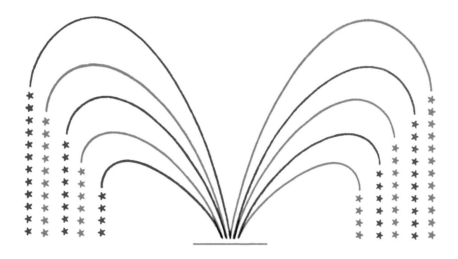

Scene III

THE SITTING-ROOM *of the Miller house again—about* 10 *o'clock the same night.* MILLER *is sitting in his rocker at left, front, of table, his wife in the rocker at right, front, of table. Moonlight shines through the screen door at right, rear. Only the green-shaded reading lamp is lit and by its light* MILLER, *his specs on, is reading a book while his wife, sewing basket in lap, is working industriously on a doily.* MRS. MILLER's *face wears an expression of unworried content.* MILLER's *face has also lost its look of harassed preoccupation, although he still is a prey to certain misgivings, when he allows himself to think of them. Several books are piled on the table by his elbow, the books that have been confiscated from* RICHARD.

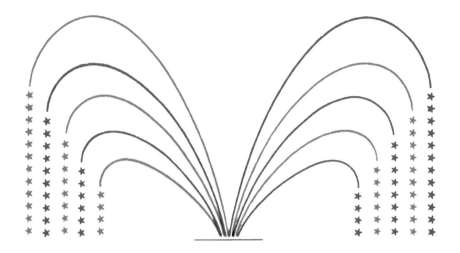

MILLER (*chuckles at something he reads—then closes the book and puts it on the table.* MRS. MILLER *looks up from her sewing*) This Shaw's a comical cuss—even if his ideas are so crazy they oughtn't to allow them to be printed. And that Swinburne's got a fine swing to his poetry—if he'd only choose some other subjects besides loose women.

MRS. MILLER (*smiling teasingly*) I can see where you're becoming corrupted by those books, too—pretending to read them out of duty to Richard, when your nose has been glued to the page!

MILLER No, no—but I've got to be honest. There's something to them. That Rubaiyat of Omar Khayyam, now. I read that over again and liked it even better than I had before—parts of it, that is, where it isn't all about boozing.

MRS. MILLER (*has been busy with her own thoughts during this last—with a deep sigh of relief*) My, but I'm glad Mildred told me where Richard went off to. I'd have worried my heart out if she hadn't. But now, it's all right.

MILLER (*frowning a little*) I'd hardly go so far as to say that. Just because we know he's all right tonight doesn't mean last night is wiped out. He's still got to be punished for that.

MRS. MILLER (*defensively*) Well, if you ask me, I think after the way I punished him all day, and the way I know he's punished himself, he's had about all he deserves. I've told you how sorry he was, and how he said he'd never touch liquor again. It didn't make him feel happy like Sid, but only sad and sick, so he didn't see anything in it for him.

MILLER Well, if he's really got that view of it driven into his skull, I don't know but I'm glad it all happened. That'll protect him more than a thousand lectures—just horse sense about himself. (*Then frowning again*) Still, I can't let him do such things and go scot-free. And then, besides, there's another side to it— (*He stops abruptly.*)

MRS. MILLER (*uneasily*) What do you mean, another side?

MILLER (*hastily*) I mean, discipline. There's got to be some discipline in a family. I don't want him to get the idea he's got a stuffed shirt at the head of the table. No, he's got to be punished, if only to make the lesson stick in his mind, and I'm going to tell him he can't go to Yale, seeing he's so undependable.

MRS. MILLER (*up in arms at once*) Not go to Yale! I guess he can go to Yale! Every man of your means in town is sending his boys to college! What would folks think of you? You let Wilbur go, and you'd have let Lawrence, only he didn't want to, and you're letting Arthur! If our other children can get the benefit of a college education, you're not going to pick on Richard—

MILLER Hush up, for God's sake! If you'd let me finish what I started to say! I said I'd *tell* him that now—bluff—then later on I'll change my mind, if he behaves himself.

MRS. MILLER Oh, well, if that's all— (*Then defensively again*) But it's your duty to give him every benefit. He's got an exceptional brain, that boy has! He's proved it by the way he likes to read all those deep plays and books and poetry.

MILLER But I thought you— (*He stops, grinning helplessly.*)

MRS. MILLER You thought I what?

MILLER Never mind.

MRS. MILLER (*sniffs, but thinks it better to let this pass*) You mark my words, that boy's going to turn out to be a great lawyer, or a great doctor, or a great writer, or—

MILLER (*grinning*) You agree he's going to be great, anyway.

MRS. MILLER Yes, I most certainly have a lot of faith in Richard.

MILLER Well, so have I, as far as that goes.

MRS. MILLER (*after a pause—judicially*) And as for his being in love with Muriel, I don't see but what it might work out real well. Richard could do worse.

MILLER But I thought you had no use for her, thought she was stupid.

MRS. MILLER Well, so I did, but if she's good for Richard and he wants her— (*Then inconsequentially*) Ma used to say you weren't over-bright, but she changed her mind when she saw I didn't care if you were or not.

MILLER (*not exactly pleased by this*) Well, I've been bright enough to—

MRS. MILLER (*going on as if he had not spoken*) And Muriel's real cute-looking, I have to admit that. Takes after her mother. Alice Briggs was the prettiest girl before she married.

MILLER Yes, and Muriel will get big as a house after she's married, the same as her mother did. That's the trouble. A man never can tell what he's letting himself in for— (*He stops, feeling his wife's eyes fixed on him with indignant suspicion.*)

MRS. MILLER *(sharply)* I'm not too fat and don't you say it!

MILLER Who was talking about you?

MRS. MILLER And I'd rather have some flesh on my bones than be built like a string bean and bore a hole in a chair every time I sat down—like some people!

MILLER *(ignoring the insult—flatteringly)* Why, no one'd ever call you fat, Essie. You're only plump, like a good figure ought to be.

MRS. MILLER *(childishly pleased—gratefully giving tit for tat)* Well, you're not skinny, either—only slender—and I think you've been putting on weight lately, too. *(Having thus squared matters she takes up her sewing again. A pause. Then MILLER asks incredulously.)*

MILLER You don't mean to tell me you're actually taking this Muriel crush of Richard's seriously, do you? I know it's a good thing to encourage right now but—pshaw, why, Richard'll probably forget all about her before he's away six months, and she'll have forgotten him.

MRS. MILLER Don't be so cynical. *(Then, after a pause, thoughtfully)* Well, anyway, he'll always have it to remember—no matter what happens after—and that's something.

MILLER You bet that's something. *(Then with a grin)* You surprise me at times with your deep wisdom.

MRS. MILLER You don't give me credit for ever having common sense, that's why. *(She goes back to her sewing.)*

MILLER *(after a pause)* Where'd you say Sid and Lily had gone off to?

MRS. MILLER To the beach to listen to the band. *(She sighs sympathetically.)* Poor Lily! Sid'll never change, and she'll never marry him. But she seems to get some queer satisfaction out of fussing over him like a hen that's hatched a duck—though Lord knows I wouldn't in her shoes!

MILLER Arthur's up with Elsie Rand, I suppose?

MRS. MILLER Of course.

MILLER Where's Mildred?

MRS. MILLER Out walking with her latest. I've forgot who it is. I can't keep track of them. (*She smiles.*)

MILLER (*smiling*) Then, from all reports, we seem to be completely surrounded by love!

MRS. MILLER Well, we've had our share, haven't we? We don't have to begrudge it to our children. (*Then has a sudden thought*) But I've done all this talking about Muriel and Richard and clean forgot how wild old McComber was against it. But he'll get over that, I suppose.

MILLER (*with a chuckle*) He has already. I ran into him upstreet this afternoon and he was meek as pie. He backed water and said he guessed I was right. Richard had just copied stuff out of books, and kids would be kids, and so on. So I came off my high horse a bit—but not too far—and I guess all that won't bother anyone any more. (*Then rubbing his hands together—with a boyish grin of pleasure*) And I told you about getting that business from Lawson, didn't I? It's been a good day, Essie—a darned good day! (*From the hall beyond the front parlor the sound of the front door being opened and shut is heard.* MRS. MILLER *leans forward to look, pushing her specs up.*)

MRS. MILLER (*in a whisper*) It's Richard.

MILLER (*immediately assuming an expression of becoming gravity*) Hmm. (*He takes off his spectacles and puts them back in their case and straightens himself in his chair.* RICHARD *comes slowly in from the front parlor. He walks like one in a trance, his eyes shining with a dreamy happiness, his spirit still too exalted to be conscious of his*

surroundings, or to remember the threatened punishment. He carries his straw hat dangling in his hand, quite unaware of its existence.)

RICHARD (*dreamily, like a ghost addressing fellow shades*) Hello.

MRS. MILLER (*staring at him worriedly*) Hello, Richard.

MILLER (*sizing him up shrewdly*) Hello, Son.
(RICHARD *moves past his mother and comes to the far corner, left front, where the light is dimmest, and sits down on the sofa, and stares before him, his hat dangling in his hand.*)

MRS. MILLER (*with frightened suspicion now*) Goodness, he acts queer! Nat, you don't suppose he's been—?

MILLER (*with a reassuring smile*) No. It's love, not liquor, this time.

MRS. MILLER (*only partly reassured—sharply*) Richard! What's the matter with you? (*He comes to himself with a start. She goes on scoldingly*) How many times have I told you to hang up your hat in the hall when you come in! (*He looks at his hat as if he were surprised at its existence. She gets up fussily and goes to him.*) Here. Give it to me. I'll hang it up for you this once. And what are you sitting over here in the dark for? Don't forget your father's been waiting to talk to you! (*She comes back to the table and he follows her, still half in a dream, and stands by his father's chair.* MRS. MILLER *starts for the hall with his hat.*)

MILLER (*quietly but firmly now*) You better leave Richard and me alone for a while, Essie.

MRS. MILLER (*turns to stare at him apprehensively*) Well—all right. I'll go sit on the piazza. Call me if you want me. (*Then a bit pleadingly*) But you'll remember all I said, Nat, won't you? (MILLER *nods reassuringly. She disappears through the front parlor.* RICHARD, *keenly conscious of himself as the about-to-be-sentenced criminal by this time, looks guilty and a bit defiant, searches his father's expressionless face with uneasy side glances, and steels himself for what is coming.)*

MILLER *(casually, indicating* MRS. MILLER'S *rocker)* Sit down, Richard. *(*RICHARD *slumps awkwardly into the chair and sits in a self-conscious, unnatural position.* MILLER *sizes him up keenly—then suddenly smiles and asks with quiet mockery)* Well, how are the vine leaves in your hair this evening?

RICHARD *(totally unprepared for this approach—shame-facedly mutters)* I don't know, Pa.

MILLER Turned out to be poison ivy, didn't they? *(Then kindly)* But you needn't look so alarmed. I'm not going to read you any temperance lecture. That'd bore me more than it would you. And, in spite of your damn foolishness last night, I'm still giving you credit for having brains. So I'm pretty sure anything I could say to you you've already said to yourself.

RICHARD *(his head down—humbly)* I know I was a darned fool.

MILLER *(thinking it well to rub in this aspect—disgustedly)* You sure were —not only a fool but a down-right, stupid, disgusting fool! *(*RICHARD *squirms, his head still lower.)* It was bad enough for you to let me and Arthur see you, but to appear like that before your mother and Mildred—! And I wonder if Muriel would think you were so fine if she ever saw you as you looked and acted then. I think she'd give you your walking papers for keeps. And you couldn't blame her. No nice girl wants to give her love to a stupid drunk!

RICHARD *(writhing)* I know, Pa.

MILLER *(after a pause—quietly)* All right. Then that settles—the booze end of it. *(He sizes* RICHARD *up searchingly—then suddenly speaks sharply.)* But there is another thing that's more serious.

How about that tart you went to bed with at the Pleasant Beach House?

RICHARD (*flabbergasted—stammers*) You know—? But I didn't! If they've told you about her down there, they must have told you I didn't! She wanted me to—but I wouldn't. I gave her the five dollars just so she'd let me out of it. Honest, Pa, I didn't! She made everything seem rotten and dirty—and—I didn't want to do a thing like that to Muriel—no matter how bad I thought she'd treated me—even after I felt drunk, I didn't. Honest!

MILLER How'd you happen to meet this lady, anyway?

RICHARD I can't tell that, Pa. I'd have to snitch on someone—and you wouldn't want me to do that.

MILLER (*a bit taken aback*) No. I suppose I wouldn't. Hmm. Well, I believe you—and I guess that settles that. (*Then, after a quick furtive glance at* RICHARD, *he nerves himself for the ordeal and begins with a shamefaced, self-conscious solemnity*) But listen here, Richard, it's about time you and I had a serious talk about —hmm—certain matters pertaining to—and now that the subject's come up of its own accord, it's a good time—I mean, there's no use in procrastinating further—so, here goes. (*But it doesn't go smoothly and as he goes on he becomes more and more guiltily embarrassed and self-conscious and his expressions more stilted.* RICHARD *sedulously avoids even glancing at him, his own embarrassment made tenfold more painful by his father's.*) Richard, you have now come to the age when— Well, you're a fully developed man, in a way, and it's only natural for you to have certain desires of the flesh, to put it that way— I mean, pertaining to the opposite sex—certain natural feelings and temptations—that'll want to be gratified—and you'll want to gratify them. Hmm—well, human society being organized as it is, there's only one outlet for—unless you're a scoundrel and go around ruining decent girls—which you're not, of course. Well, there are a certain class of women—always have been and always will be as long as human nature is what it is— It's wrong, maybe, but what can you do about it? I mean, girls like that one you—girls there's something doing with—and lots of 'em are pretty, and it's human nature if you— But that doesn't mean to ever get mixed up with them seriously! You just have what you want and pay 'em and forget it. I know that sounds hard and unfeeling, but we're talking facts and— But don't think I'm encouraging you to— If you can stay away from 'em, all the better—but if—why—hmm— Here's what I'm driving at, Richard. They're apt to be whited sepulchres— I mean, your whole life might be ruined if—so, darn it, you've got to know how to— I mean, there are ways and means— (*Suddenly he can go no farther and winds up helplessly*) But, hell, I suppose you boys talk all this over among yourselves and you know more about it than I do. I'll admit I'm no authority. I never had anything to do with such women, and it'll be a hell of a lot better for you if you never do!

RICHARD   (*without looking at him*) I'm never going to, Pa. (*Then shocked indignation coming into his voice*) I don't see how you could think I could—now—when you know I love Muriel and am going to marry her. I'd die before I'd—!

MILLER   (*immensely relieved—enthusiastically*) That's the talk! By God, I'm proud of you when you talk like that! (*Then hastily*) And now that's all of that. There's nothing more to say and we'll forget it, eh?

RICHARD   (*after a pause*) How are you going to punish me, Pa?

MILLER   I was sort of forgetting that, wasn't I? Well, I'd thought of telling you you couldn't go to Yale—

RICHARD (*eagerly*) Don't I have to go? Gee, that's great! Muriel thought you'd want me to. I was telling her I'd rather you gave me a job on the paper because then she and I could get married sooner. (*Then with a boyish grin*) Gee, Pa, you picked a lemon. That isn't any punishment. You'll have to do something besides that.

MILLER (*grimly—but only half concealing an answering grin*) Then you'll go to Yale and you'll stay there till you graduate, that's the answer to that! Muriel's got good sense and you haven't! (RICHARD *accepts this philosophically.*) And now we're finished, you better call your mother. (RICHARD *opens the screen door and calls "Ma," and a moment later she comes in. She glances quickly from son to husband and immediately knows that all is well and tactfully refrains from all questions.*)

MRS. MILLER My, it's a beautiful night. The moon's way down low—almost setting. (*She sits in her chair and sighs contentedly.* RICHARD *remains standing by the door, staring out at the moon, his face pale in the moonlight.*)

MILLER (*with a nod at* RICHARD, *winking at his wife*) Yes, I don't believe I've hardly ever seen such a beautiful night—with such a wonderful moon. Have you, Richard?

RICHARD (*turning to them—enthusiastically*) No! It was wonderful— down at the beach— (*He stops abruptly, smiling shyly.*)

MILLER (*watching his son—after a pause—quietly*) I can only remember a few nights that were as beautiful as this—and they were so long ago, when your mother and I were young and planning to get married.

RICHARD (*stares at him wonderingly for a moment, then quickly from his father to his mother and back again, strangely, as if he'd never seen them before—then he looks almost disgusted and swallows as if an acrid taste had come into his mouth—but then suddenly his face is transfigured by a smile of shy understanding and sympathy. He speaks shyly)* Yes, I'll bet those must have been wonderful nights, too. You sort of forget the moon was the same way back then—and everything.

MILLER *(huskily)* You're all right, Richard. *(He gets up and blows his nose.)*

MRS. MILLER *(fondly)* You're a good boy, Richard. *(RICHARD looks dreadfully shy and embarrassed at this. His father comes to his rescue.)*

MILLER Better get to bed early tonight, Son, hadn't you?

RICHARD I couldn't sleep. Can't I go out on the piazza and sit for a while—until the moon sets?

MILLER All right. Then you better say good night now. I don't know about your mother, but I'm going to bed right away. I'm dead tired.

MRS. MILLER So am I.

RICHARD *(goes to her and kisses her)* Good night, Ma.

MRS. MILLER Good night. Don't you stay up till all hours now.

RICHARD *(comes to his father and stands awkwardly before him)* Good night, Pa.

MILLER *(puts his arm around him and gives him a hug)* Good night, Richard. *(RICHARD turns impulsively and kisses him—then hurries out the screen door. MILLER stares after him—then says huskily)* First time he's done that in years. I don't believe in kissing between fathers and sons after a certain age—seems mushy and silly—but that meant something! And I don't think we'll ever have to worry about his being safe—from himself—again. And I guess no matter what life will do to him, he can take care of it now. *(He sighs with satisfaction and, sitting down*

in his chair, begins to unlace his shoes.) My darned feet are giving me fits!

MRS. MILLER   *(laughing)* Why do you bother unlacing your shoes now, you big goose—when we're going right up to bed?

MILLER   *(as if he hadn't thought of that before, stops)* Guess you're right. *(Then getting to his feet—with a grin)* Mind if I don't say my prayers tonight, Essie? I'm certain God knows I'm too darned tired.

MRS. MILLER   Don't talk that way. It's real sinful. *(She gets up—then laughing fondly)* If that isn't you all over! Always looking for an excuse to— You're worse than Tommy! But all right. I suppose tonight you needn't. You've had a hard day. *(She puts her hand on the reading-lamp switch.)* I'm going to turn out the light. All ready?

MILLER   Yep. Let her go, Gallagher. *(She turns out the lamp. In the ensuing darkness the faint moonlight shines full in through the screen door. Walking together toward the front parlor they stand full in it for a moment, looking out.* MILLER *puts his arm around her. He says in a low voice)* There he is—like a statue of Love's Young Dream. *(Then he sighs and speaks with a gentle nostalgic melancholy)* What's it that Rubaiyat says:

"Yet Ah, that Spring should vanish with the Rose!
That Youth's sweet-scented manuscript should close!"

(Then throwing off his melancholy, with a loving smile at her) Well, Spring isn't everything, is it, Essie? There's a lot to be said for Autumn. That's got beauty, too. And Winter—if you're together.

MRS. MILLER   *(simply)* Yes, Nat. *(She kisses him and they move quietly out of the moonlight, back into the darkness of the front parlor.)*

Curtain